VOCAL CHAMBER MUSIC

RECENT RESEARCHES IN THE MUSIC OF THE BAROQUE ERA

Robert L. Marshall, general editor

A-R Editions, Inc., publishes six quarterly series—

Recent Researches in the Music of the Middle Ages and Early Renaissance
Margaret Bent, general editor

Recent Researches in the Music of the Renaissance
James Haar, general editor

Recent Researches in the Music of the Baroque Era
Robert L. Marshall, general editor

Recent Researches in the Music of the Classical Era
Eugene K. Wolf, general editor

Recent Researches in the Music of the Nineteenth and Early Twentieth Centuries
Rufus Hallmark, general editor

Recent Researches in American Music
H. Wiley Hitchcock, general editor—

which make public music that is being brought to light
in the course of current musicological research.

Each volume in the *Recent Researches* is devoted
to works by a single composer or to a single genre of composition,
chosen because of its potential interest to scholars and performers,
and prepared for publication according to the standards that govern
the making of all reliable historical editions.

Subscribers to this series, as well as patrons of subscribing institutions,
are invited to apply for information about the "Copyright-Sharing Policy"
of A-R Editions, Inc., under which the contents of this volume
may be reproduced free of charge for study or performance.

Correspondence should be addressed:

A-R EDITIONS, INC.
315 West Gorham Street
Madison, Wisconsin 53703

RECENT RESEARCHES IN THE MUSIC OF THE BAROQUE ERA • VOLUME XLVIII

Marc-Antoine Charpentier

VOCAL CHAMBER MUSIC

Edited by John S. Powell

A-R EDITIONS, INC. • MADISON

Library of Congress Cataloging in Publication Data

Charpentier, Marc Antoine, 1634–1704.
  [Vocal music. Selections]
  Vocal chamber music.

  (Recent researches in the music of the baroque era,
ISSN 0484–0828 ; v. 48)
  1. Vocal music. I. Powell, John S. II. Series.
M2.R238   vol. 48   [M3.1]   84–760235
ISBN 0–89579–202–8

Contents

Preface

This volume contains seven vocal chamber works which are classified as secular cantatas in H. Wiley Hitchcock, *Les oeuvres de Marc-Antoine Charpentier: Catalogue raisonné.*[1] This important but neglected music historically occupies a midpoint between the Roman cantatas of Luigi Rossi, Marco Marazzoli, and Giacomo Carissimi of the mid-seventeenth century, and the 1706 publication of Jean-Baptiste Morin's first book of *Cantates françoises à une et deux voix melées de symphonies.* Four of these seven works, *Cantate françoise de M. Charpentier, Superbo amore, Il mondo così và,* and *Beate mie pene* resemble the single-movement cantata form common in Italy before 1670—short ariettes for one or two voices with continuo set in binary, ternary, rounded binary, or rondo form. *Orphée descendant aux enfers* and *Epitaphium Carpentarij,* on the other hand, look forward to the multisectional cantata of the late seventeenth and early eighteenth centuries in which the distinction between recitative and aria styles becomes clearer, and in which the recitative occupies a smaller proportion of the cantata, while the arias and ensembles expand into longer, self-contained movements.[2] The *Serenata a tre voci e simphonia* occupies a middle ground between the single-movement arietta and the "numbers cantata." Wholly without sectional divisions, the work is an extended movement composed of episodes of motto-prelude, chorus, and solo—all following one another without breaks and employing constant elision between episodes of different instrumental and vocal media.

In all, these chamber works by one of the indisputable giants of the French baroque present an interesting and unique blend of early- and late-seventeenth-century Italian styles and forms.

The Composer

Although Marc-Antoine Charpentier was second only to Lully as the most prominent musical personality in late-seventeenth-century Paris, few authoritative documents pertaining to him have come down to us, and our knowledge of his life and musical career is therefore sketchy.[3] Relatively little is known about the years prior to 1672, when Charpentier suddenly burst upon the Parisian musical scene, replacing Lully as the composer for Molière's Troupe du Roy. According to many sources Charpentier was born in Paris,[4] but the date of his birth remains uncertain.[5] Of Charpentier's early musical education we know little. He studied in Rome[6] for a time with Giacomo Carissimi (1605–74), who was musical director at the Jesuit Collegium Germanicum.[7] While in Rome, Charpentier also associated with the bohemian poet-musician Charles Coypeau (*dit* Dassoucy, 1605–77), who is known to have resided in Rome in the mid-1660s.[8]

Upon his return to Paris (ca. 1670) Charpentier was eventually employed by both the troupe of Molière and the Maîson de Guise.[9] Marie de Lorraine, the Duchesse de Guise (1615–88), was one of the leading private patrons of music, and, according to the *Mercure galant,* the quality of her musical establishment was "so good that it could be said that those of many great monarchs did not rival it."[10] Charpentier served as her *maître de musique* and composer in residence until her death in 1688.[11] During these years Charpentier wrote secular dramatic works, sacred motets, oratorios, and psalm settings—in which he occasionally sang *haute-contre* parts—for her musical soirées and religious services.[12]

The earliest documentation of Charpentier as a composer begins with his association with the Troupe du Roy, when he collaborated with Molière in the Parisian premiere of *La comtesse d'Escarbagnas* (8 July 1672).[13] For this production Molière replaced Lully's original divertissement, *Le ballet des ballets* (presented at the court premiere of *La comtesse d'Escarbagnas* in December of 1671), with a new musical version of *Le mariage forcé* including *intermèdes* by Charpentier.[14] Although Molière's death during the first run of his *Malade imaginaire* (another play for which Charpentier had composed the music) in February of 1673 prematurely concluded their personal collaboration, Charpentier remained until 1695 as the official composer for what had been Molière's theatrical troupe, which became, in 1680, the Comédie-Française.[15]

In the early 1680s Charpentier was appointed director of the musical entourage of Louis, the Grand Dauphin (1661–1711), for whom he wrote dramatic works on courtly subjects and sacred motets. According to the *Mercure galant,* the king took a special interest in Charpentier's music:

> Upon arriving at Saint-Cloud, the King dismissed all of his musical entourage and wished to hear that of Monseigneur le Dauphin until his return to Saint-Germain. The King heard sung every day at Mass some motets by Monsieur Charpentier, and His Majesty would hear no others, regardless of what was proposed to him.[16]

Charpentier entered the open competition for one of the four newly created posts of *sous-maître* of the royal chapel in the spring of 1683, but he was forced to withdraw due to illness.[17] However, two months later Charpentier was granted a royal pension, either as a consolation prize or, more likely, in reward for his services to the Grand Dauphin.[18]

In the mid-1680s Charpentier served as *maître de musique* and composer to the Jesuit church of St. Louis (later named St. Paul-St. Louis), for which he wrote a large number of religious works. The Jesuit Collège de Clermont (also known as Louis-le-Grand) commissioned Charpentier to write musical settings of the sacred dramas *Celse Martyr* (MS lost) and *David et Jonathas* (H. 490), and for the Jesuit Collège d'Harcourt he provided musical *intermèdes* for Corneille's sacred drama *Polieucte* (H. 498). On 18 June 1698 Charpentier was appointed to the post of *maître de musique* of the Sainte-Chapelle du Palais, which had fallen vacant with the death of the previous musical director, François Chaperon.[19] Charpentier remained in this prestigious position—second in church music only to the directorship of the royal chapel at Versailles—until his death on 24 February 1704.

The Music

Charpentier's extant music consists primarily of occasional works written (or, in some cases, rearranged from previous works) in connection with one of the five musical posts he occupied during his active career. The bulk of his repertoire is sacred music—masses, motets, and psalm-settings—composed for Parisian churches, for the private chapels of the Duchesse de Guise and of the Dauphin, for the Jesuit churches and colleges, for various convents and abbeys, and for the Sainte-Chapelle du Palais. Next most numerous are his theatrical works, both sacred and secular, which include: pastorales, tragedies, and dramatic cantatas for the Duchesse de Guise; Latin plays and religious operas for the Jesuit colleges; prologues, *intermèdes*, and incidental music written for the Comédie-Française; and *Médée* (H. 491), a *tragédie-lyrique* premiered at the Académie Royale de Musique (4 December 1693). Finally, there is a small group of chamber works written for diverse vocal and instrumental ensembles.

The works selected for this edition (nos. 471–72 and 474–78 in Hitchcock's *Catalogue raisonné*) are drawn from this last category.[20] Although none can be specifically dated, these cantata-like works were most likely composed for various occasions spanning Charpentier's musical career (which lasted from ca. 1672 to ca. 1702).[21] Pieces included in this edition demonstrate a diversity of styles and genres, ranging from arietta and chamber duet through secular oratorio, and thereby they establish a direct link between the early Italian solo cantata and the later French *cantate françoise*.

One of the works specifically dated in the *Catalogue raisonné* is the dramatic cantata *Orphée descendant aux enfers* (H. 471),[22] for which Hitchcock provides (without explanation) the date 1683.[23] Scored for *haute-contre*, tenor, and bass voices, along with an instrumental ensemble of two violins, recorder, transverse flute, and *basse continüe*, *Orphée descendant aux enfers* utilizes the same musical forces as were in the permanent employ of the Duchesse de Guise at the time when Charpentier served as her *maître de musique*.[24] One of the violins (*premier dessus*) in the instrumental prelude is designated "viollon d'Orphée" (see Plate I) and is accorded a solo *récit* prior to the first air ("Effroyables enfers"); no doubt this violin part was played by whoever sang the role of Orphée; Quittard suggests this may have been Charpentier himself.[25] Some authors speculate that this cantata, due to its

brevity, is either unfinished or lost in part;[26] however, this is doubtful. *Orphée descendant aux enfers* is proportionate in length to later cantatas of the eighteenth century, and its continuous dramatic action, concerning only the portion of the myth in which Orpheus enters the Kingdom of Hades, precisely fits the composer's title. The unique, autograph source manuscript (F-Pn, Rés. Vm[1] 259, VI, fols. 11–16) is foliated in consecutive numbers and the movements progress in logical sequence, so that any missing music would have to have occurred at the beginning or at the end. Since the title appears on the first folio of the manuscript and the inscription "fin" (along with the composer's measure-count) appears on the final folio, one must conclude that the cantata is a complete work as it stands; the hypothesis that any portion is missing or that it is part of a larger work (such as the incomplete opera on the same subject, *La descente d'Orphée aux enfers* [H. 488]) is unsubstantiated.[27]

Orphée descendant aux enfers is the only chamber work in this edition devoted to a mythological subject, the legend of Orpheus and Eurydice. The author of the text is unidentified, though he might possibly have been the librettist of *La descente d'Orphée aux enfers*—which was also written and performed at the Maîson de Guise during Charpentier's tenure as *maître de musique*. There are no known musical settings of this cantata text by other composers.

Orphée descendant aux enfers is clearly a sectional piece in which "movements" are delineated by the composer's own directions for articulative pauses ("faites icy un petit silence" [p. 15], "faites icy une petite pause" [p. 16]) as well as an indication to continue without pause ("passez sans interruption au récit d'Orphée sur le viollon" [p. 5]). These instructions directed to the performers prove that Charpentier regarded silence between movements as an essential part of the dramatic effect.

This cantata presents a stylistic dualism of French and Italian musical traits: its orchestration is the heavy, five-part texture of traditional French operatic accompaniment, while its rich harmonic language is highlighted by affective intervals and angular melodic leaps common to the Italian repertory. The *Prélude*, which hints at tripartite form with its initial dotted rhythms and upbeat *tirades* (mm. 1–13) followed by passages of imitative entries (mm. 14–41) and a return to the dotted rhythms of the opening (mm. 41–57), bears many traits common to the *ouverture à la française*. By its orderly succession of instrumental preludes and postludes, its alternation of recitative-like passages with measured airs, and by its moralizing lyrics of the concluding movement, *Orphée descendant aux enfers* clearly foreshadows the mature French chamber cantata of the early eighteenth century.

Cantate françoise de M. Charpentier (H. 478) appears in a single manuscript source (MS 1182, pp. 25–32) contained in the Bibliothèque Municipale, Musée Calvet, in Avignon. Copied in an eighteenth-century hand, this score was apparently compiled from separate instrumental and vocal parts (notice the error listed in the Critical Notes for mm. 17–28, where the *basse continüe* has been miscopied). *Cantate françoise de M. Charpentier* has been frequently cited as an early example of the French cantata,[28] but only recently has its attribution to Marc-Antoine Charpentier been called into question. It is listed in Hitchcock's *Catalogue raisonné*, where the author states, "the attribution to Charpentier is of doubtful authenticity: the style of the work, extremely Italianate, seems to postdate that of Charpentier."[29] Anthony questions these extremely Italianate features and suggests that its French traits stylistically outweigh the Italian.[30] Although he had once accepted Marc-Antoine Charpentier as the composer,[31] Anthony now speculates that the cantata "more likely . . . stems from one of the Avignon Charpentiers, one of whom was identified . . . as Charpentier 'l'aîné' who collaborated with Bertrand Ranc and Claude Jullien between 1682 and 1700 in composing ballets for the Jesuit College."[32]

Cantate françoise de M. Charpentier, scored for tenor voice, two violins, and continuo, utilizes the idiomatic string writing of a trio-sonata to support the voice (in sharp contrast to the thicker five-part instrumental texture of *Orphée descendant aux enfers*), which, along with the "motto" beginning, must count among its Italianate features.[33] But its melodic style is decidedly French—consisting of a lyricism that avoids angular contours while moving with the graceful gestures of the dance, and in which the nuances of the French words become highlighted by means of delicate ornamentation.[34] *Cantate françoise de M. Charpentier* certainly does not sound like other works by Marc-Antoine: many of the composer's well-known trademarks (affective melodic intervals and vertical cross-relations, dissonant harmonic clashes between instrumental parts at cadences, chains of 7–6 suspensions) are noticeably absent. While its authenticity is highly doubtful, *Cantate françoise de M. Charpentier* has been included in this edition primarily because it is, next to *Orphée descendant aux enfers*, the most frequently cited example of the French cantata in the seventeenth century (see n. 28); once made available for study and performance, its attribution can be more widely considered.

The author of the undistinguished pastoral text of *Cantate françoise de M. Charpentier* is unidentified, and there are no known settings of this text by other composers. Unlike the typical multisectional cantata of the early eighteenth century, *Cantate françoise de M. Charpentier* resembles the earlier Italian arietta-cantata, consisting more or less of a single aria. It is set in ternary form, in which the similar outer sections are contrasted with a middle section in arioso style (mm. 58–85). At the beginning of this middle section the meter changes to 3 and then almost immediately back again to ¢. This ternary structure is further articulated by the obbligato violins, which are silent during the middle section. Although the obbligato writing does make some use of imitative points, these are not pursued at any length, and for the most part the texture is homophonic.

The unique source for the *Serenata a tre voci e simphonia*[35] (H. 472), notated in Charpentier's characteristic hand (see Plate II), is scored for three-part chorus; soprano, alto *(haute-contre)*, and bass soli; two unspecified treble instruments; and *basse continüe*. In his *Catalogue raisonné* Hitchcock dates the work "ca. 1685,"[36] presum-

ably based on its location within the composer's *Mélanges autographes* contained in the Bibliothèque Nationale, Paris (F-Pn, Rés. Vm¹ 259, VII, fols. 18–24ᵛ). Gastoué lists the *Serenata* among Charpentier's theatrical works and states, "it is distinct from the 'Serenade' for [Molière's] *Le Sicilien*," but there is no evidence, literary or musical, that indicates it is part of a theatrical presentation.[37] Most likely, this Italian *divertimento* was intended for the private entertainment of the Duchesse de Guise, the Duc d'Orléans, or one of Charpentier's other musical patrons.

Traditionally, the *serenata* (or *serenada*) of the sixteenth century was a performance with voices and instruments in a lady's honor which took place in the evening *(la sera)*—usually beneath her window. In the later seventeenth century the term became used for semi-dramatic cantatas in several movements that were performed by a small orchestra and several singers. The subject matter was mythological, pastoral, or allegorical, and the staging often entailed elaborate scenery and sumptuous costumes (e.g., Stradella's *Qual prodigio e ch'io miri*, borrowed by Handel in *Israel in Egypt*). Charpentier's *Serenata a tre voci e simphonia* is an extended, cantata-like work that begins with an instrumental prelude and continues with vocal ensembles for chorus and soli, all interspersed with instrumental ritornelli. But unlike the *serenatas* of Stradella, Alessandro Scarlatti, and Handel, Charpentier's work progresses in one continuous, through-composed movement. Its anonymous Italian text is akin to sixteenth-century *serenatas* in that it is an exhortation to weary lovers (sung by the chorus) and a presentation of three examples (sung by the solo parts in turn) of correct conduct for the edification of those who would love well.

The *Serenata a tre voci e simphonia* is a supremely Italianate chamber work. The prelude, ritornelli, and accompaniment utilize the instrumentation of the Italian trio-sonata, and in both form and orchestral procedures (which contrast the instrumental with the vocal forces, both choral and solo, in continually changing combinations), the work employs techniques of *concerto-grosso* composition. Examples of descriptive word-painting are legion: long-held notes for "lunghi pianti" (lengthy plaints); breathless falling leaps for "sospirate" (sigh); passionate melismatic florishes for "ardete" (burn); melismatic excursions for "cercando" (I seek); a high note for "sole" (sun); and a held note for "immortal" (unending). The beginning and ending choruses (mm. 17–62 and mm. 157–90), in fact, resemble the continuo madrigal. These choruses employ imitative points among the instruments, among the choral parts, between the instruments and choral parts, and, in the solo sections, between instruments and solo voices. Each of the solos introduces the "motto" beginning common to Italian cantata and opera arias of the late seventeenth and early eighteenth centuries. In text and text-setting, instrumentation, use of concerto techniques and concerto-like formal principles, madrigalesque sections for choruses and motto arias for soloists, Charpentier's *Serenata a tre voci e simphonia* is a compendium of mid-seventeenth-century Italian compositional techniques.

Superbo amore (H. 476) and *Il mondo così và* (H. 477) survive together in a single three-page manuscript, in which *Superbo amore* is notated across the top and *Il mondo così và* across the bottom of each sheet (see Plate III). The unidentified copyist of this source (F-Pn, Vm⁷ 18, pp. 70–72) inscribed "di Charpentiers" preceding the score of the former work, and "di Char." preceding the latter. These chamber works bear no clues pertaining to date or provenance of composition.

Superbo amore, scored for soprano, contralto, and *basse continüe*, resembles the earlier Italian arietta-cantata popular among Roman cantata composers during the mid-seventeenth century. Consisting of a single strophe of verse, the anonymous text is musically set in binary form with the sections demarked by a double barline; there is, however, a suggestion of tripartite structure since imitation between the voices appears at the beginning (mm. 1–15) and end (mm. 32–50), while the central portion (mm. 16–31) is predominantly homophonic.

Il mondo così và, scored for soprano solo and *basse continüe*, is another binary arietta but with a more complicated musical/poetic structure. The anonymous text is a cynical diatribe in which the first strophe attacks love in general, and the second attacks women in particular. The last line of each strophe ends "imparate a mie spese, ô folli amanti!" (learn at my expense, o foolish lovers!), which functions as a literary and musical refrain (mm. 28–40). The first part of the binary division (mm. 1–15) is itself set in rounded binary form, and it repeats the music and words "il mondo così và" (so goes the world) in mm. 12–15, before the double barlines. In both compositional techniques and musical structure, *Superbo amore* and *Il mondo così và* prove themselves to be brief but carefully crafted works which owe an unmistakable debt to earlier Italian cantata-models.

The Bibliothèque Nationale owns two copies (neither of which is an autograph) of the chamber duet *Beate mie pene* (H. 475). The provenance and dates of these manuscripts are unknown. The source used for transcription here is a score entitled "a 2ᵉ del Sʳ Charpentier" (F-Pn, Vm⁷ 53, pp. 74–77). Notated in an elegant hand, this score was perhaps intended as a presentation copy since many performance details are omitted; however, it offers the more accurate reading of the musical and literary text. A hastily written set of performing parts for two sopranos and *basse continüe* (F-Pn, Vm⁷ 8, fols. 17–20) bears the titles "Beate mie Pené: Duo a doi canti del Sign. Charpentier" (fol. 17, title page) and "Aria del Sign Charpentier a doi canti" (fol. 17ᵛ, soprano parts). The parts include more ornaments, continuo figures, and dynamic markings than the score version, and these performance indications have been added in the present edition to augment those transcribed from the score.

The author of this rather conventional love poetry is unidentified, and the text is not known to have been set by other composers. Whereas this text is notated in correct Italian in the score version (Vm⁷ 53) used for this transcription, the soprano performing parts (Vm⁷ 8) provide phonetic spellings of many words—*piou* for *più, ki* for *chi, felitchi* for *felici, laschiate* for *lasciate*, and *croudel'* for *crudeli* (presumably for the linguistic benefit of French-

speaking singers). Furthermore, elided syllables set to one note in the score are given two notes in the parts version for the phrase "non gode in amor."

The text consists of a single strophe of verse, extended by repetition and set to music in a single continuous movement. The musical structure is tripartite: the first section (mm. 1–51) employs conventional Italianate word-painting, with melismatic interweavings on the words *catene* (chains) and *legami* (bonds); in the second section, points of imitation between the equal voices are vigorously pursued in the setting of the remainder of the text (mm. 51–77, where a quicker tempo is editorially suggested); the final section (mm. 77–117) sets a repetition of the entire text in a kind of variation in which the imitative vocal entrances are reversed (compare mm. 51–59/87–95 and mm. 65–73/95–105) and are followed by a short passage of voice exchange (mm. 105–13) that, in turn, is followed by a hushed homophonic repetition of the final phrase (mm. 113–17). The form, compositional procedure, and style of *Beate mie pene* resemble those of Rossi's and Carissimi's duet-cantatas, with which Charpentier surely became acquainted while studying in Rome. The composer's debt to these Italian models is apparent in his choice of text (Italian love poetry), text-setting (with Italianate madrigalisms), performance medium (two equal soprano voices with continuo), and a vocal texture consisting primarily of imitative entries uniting in euphonic parallel thirds.

Epitaphium Carpentarij (H. 474), for *haute-contre*, tenor, bass, a trio of treble voices, and *basse continüe*, is a secular counterpart to Charpentier's Latin oratorios. It survives in a unique, autograph manuscript now held by the Bibliothèque Nationale (F-Pn, Rés. Vm¹ 259, XIII, fols. 60ᵛ–65). The text is written in Latin, partly in prose and partly in verse, and, considering its autobiographical nature, it may well be by the composer himself. *Epitaphium Carpentarij* (Funeral Oration of Charpentier) is a peculiar work—humorous, devastatingly satiric and punning, but at the same time a trifle melancholic—in which the composer's spirit (Umbra Carpentarij) returns to earth to announce:

> I was a musician, considered among the good musicians by the good, and among the ignorant musicians by the ignorant. And since more numerous were those who scorned me than those who praised me, music became a small honor and a heavy burden; and just as I, when born, brought nothing into this world, thus, when dying, I took nothing away.

Later, the spirit ridicules the music of François Chaperon—Charpentier's predecessor at the Sainte-Chapelle du Palais:[38]

> Ah, comrades, he who held the name of Carissimi while on earth is called Chaperon in heaven. . . .[39] Repent and embrace this music of Chaperon; choose for yourself this music as punishment and purgatory, and after death you will taste the joys of eternal life. . . . Blessed is he who, to purge his sins, will tire, castigate, and chaperonize his ears with disgusting and discordant chaperonian, [i.e., goatish] music. . . . Blessed is he who, to purge his sins, will patiently listen to the asinine hack-work of Chaperon.

The barbs Charpentier's spirit directs at Chaperon, along with the mature musical style, suggest that *Epitaphium Carpentarij* was composed late in Charpentier's career.[40] Possibly, this musical lampoon was designed to humorously discredit the former *maître de musique* of the Sainte-Chapelle after Charpentier assumed his position in June 1698 (one month following Chaperon's death). The spirit indicates that *Epitaphium Carpentarij* was performed prior to the turn of the century ("I am he who was born long ago and had been known widely during this century . . ."), so by means of textual evidence it appears safe to assume the work was written and performed sometime between 1698 and 1700.[41]

Epitaphium Carpentarij is a cantata-like work in no fewer than eleven movements varying in length from nine to ninety-two measures. Few instrumental passages or performance directions appear in the score to help articulate the musical structure, which often proceeds without break from solo sections to duets and trios. While the distinction between recitative and aria is generally clear, the two are frequently blended and juxtaposed at the promptings of the text: a recitative may become more lyrical and be almost imperceptibly transformed into an extended section in aria style (mm. 272–300), or an aria-like passage (mm. 92–109) may end with a brief recitative (mm. 110–18). The predominant solo style might best be described as free-form arioso, such as that found in the Italian arietta-cantata of the mid-seventeenth century. While some of the features associated with the aria are present (triple meter, text-repetition, melodic sequence), the solos do not take on the formal structure of arias.

On the other hand, the vocal ensembles of *Epitaphium Carpentarij* are highly organized, self-contained movements. The three duets involving Ignatius and Marcellus (mm. 10–20, 82–92, and 257–71) feature imitation between the voices, which dissolves into homophonic texture at the ends of phrases. The text-setting is mostly declamatory and syllabic, but there are descriptive melismas on "fugiamus" (let us flee) and "volabis" (fly). The five vocal trios are brief, motet-like works in a variety of forms: A–A' (mm. 50–69 and 362–91), A–B (mm. 226–56), and A–B–A (mm. 134–225 and 301–54). Unification is achieved in these trios by the use of imitative points and tonal organization. The "Cantique des Anges," a trio for treble voices and continuo, is a high point both musically and structurally and occupies a prominent central position in the work.

Editorial Methods

The primary editorial concern is to achieve a musical rendition that will permit the scholar to reconstruct the original sources and that will at the same time serve the purposes of the performer. To this end, a simple realization of the *basse continüe* is provided (upon which the knowledgeable performer can elaborate), and any discrepancies between the original manuscripts (including concordant sources) and the edition are documented in the Critical Notes. Portions of the original manuscripts are frequently in a condensed score form, with as many as four instrumental parts written on a single staff: such condensations have been expanded here, with a separate staff provided for each instrumental and vocal part. Specific verbal instructions that bear directly upon the musical performance (e.g., "faites icy une petite pause") or pertain to aspects of staging (e.g., "trois anges qu'on entend et qu'on ne voit point") frequently appear in the sources and are included in the present edition. Instrumental instructions (e.g., "flûtes seules") are retained whenever pertinent to the musical performance; when redundant or misleading, these directions have been omitted from the music and described in the Critical Notes.

Old spellings of the texts (and the verbal directions) are retained, but punctuation, capitalization, and diacritical marks have been added editorially, where necessary, without documentation. Word hyphenation has been modernized throughout the text. When the original source indicates repeated text by means of the symbol ☰, the text has been editorially added and placed within brackets. Similarly, abbreviated words are spelled out and the added letters bracketed. Apostrophes are used within the sources to indicate contractions of two words (e.g., *l'amour*) and to signify elision of two syllables (e.g., *descendre'aux*); these two usages are distinguished in the underlaid text of the edition by retaining the apostrophe in contractions and by replacing the apostrophe with an inverted semicircle between the two syllables of an elision.

Vocal parts in the sources indicate three classifications of male and female voices by the following clefs and ranges:

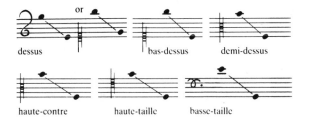

These voice types correspond, respectively, to the modern soprano, mezzo-soprano, female alto, male alto, tenor, and bass classifications. Original voice-part labels have been retained in the edition. Modern G-clefs are used in the edition for all female voice-parts, and transposing G-clefs and F-clefs are used for the male voice-parts. One ambiguous classification is the gender of the alto part in *Serenata a tre voci e simphonia*, which could have been intended for either a male or a female alto—though the range suggests an *haute-contre* by its low tessitura. This particular alto part has been transcribed here in non-transposing G-clef. The edition gives an incipit showing the original clef, key signature, meter symbol, and first note at the initial appearance of every vocal and instrumental part.

Obbligato instruments in the sources all employ the French violin clef 𝄞, for which a modern G-clef has been substituted. The only continuo instrument specified is the *viole* (i.e., *basse de viole*) in *Orphée descendant aux enfers*. (Note the quadruple stop, m. 283.) The *viole* was probably combined here with a harpsichord or theorbo to fill in the continuo harmonies. When present, the continuo figuration in the sources is often sketchy, occasionally erroneous, and usually inconsistently positioned in relation to the bass line and the vertical harmonies implied by the upper parts. In the edition, these figures have been placed below the bass line and aligned with the harmonic changes of the upper parts. Whereas in the original figures, flat inflections indicate minor or diminished intervals and sharps major or augmented intervals, in the edition these are tacitly modernized to correspond with the actual inflection of the realized pitches.

The music is transcribed in the notational style most familiar to modern readers. Repeated accidentals within the measure are omitted, and canceling sharps and flats are replaced by naturals. Editorially added accidentals appear in brackets, and cautionaries are in parentheses. The number of eighth- and sixteenth-notes beamed together has been regularized in accordance with modern practice. The idiosyncratic white eighth-notes *(croches blanches)* and white sixteenth-notes of the sources are rendered here as quarter-notes and eighth-notes, respectively. Less troublesome to the modern user are the original metric symbols and the *longa* and *breve* note-shapes, and these have been retained in the present edition.

The sectional character of *Orphée descendant aux enfers* and *Epitaphium Carpentarij* has been discussed above. In *Orphée descendant aux enfers*, each section begins with a heading (to which editorial additions have been made) and ends with a thin-thick double barline. In *Epitaphium Carpentarij* each major movement concludes with thin-thin double barlines, editorially introduced in the edition and documented in the Critical Notes when absent in the original source.

Notes on Performance

Three of these chamber works *(Orphée descendant aux enfers, Cantate françoise de M. Charpentier,* and *Serenata a tre voci e simphonia)* are scored for obbligato instruments along with the continuo accompaniment. Only *Orphée descendant aux enfers* provides clues regarding the number of performers intended on each instrumental part: the instrumental designations provided at the beginning of the *Prélude* label four instruments *(viollon d'Orph[ée], flûte à bec, fl[ûte] allem[ande],* and *viole)* in the singular (Plate I), and there are no indications that the parts should be doubled. The other works with obbligato instruments would probably also employ one instrument per part. The only continuo instrument specified in these works is the *viole* (i.e., *basse de viole*) of *Orphée descendant aux enfers*, which no doubt doubled the left-hand of the harpsichord part—the instrument most likely used for continuo realization.[42] A single theorbo could be substituted for the harpsichord in the solo arietta and chamber duets *(Il mondo così và, Superbo amore, Beate mie pene)*, but more likely the harpsichord would have been used in conjunction with obbligato instruments in *Cantate françoise de M. Charpentier* and *Serenata a tre voci e simphonia*. Considering the

mock-religious nature of *Epitaphium Carpentarij*, an organ and bassoon might be the best choice (with a harp accompanying the "Cantique des Anges").

There is little doubt that the semi-dramatic works *(Orphée descendant aux enfers* and *Epitaphium Carpentarij)*, the solo cantata and arietta *(Cantate françoise de M. Charpentier* and *Il mondo così và)*, and the chamber duets *(Superbo amore* and *Beate mie pene)* were intended for performance by solo voices. The *Serenata a tre voci e simphonia*, on the other hand, begins with a section marked "Choro" (m. 17). Voice parts for this work are notated in soprano, alto (or *haute-contre*), and bass clefs and were probably doubled with two or three singers on a part. Beginning with m. 64, the music is no doubt intended for solo voices until m. 157, where the chorus presumably returns.

Four symbols of ornamentation appear in the manuscript sources: ⌣ , ⌣⌣ , +, and ⌣ . Only the first two are found within the composer's autographs. The symbol ⌣ occurs most frequently attached to notes of relatively brief duration and is probably best interpreted as a short trill beginning with the upper auxiliary. The symbol ⌣⌣ appears attached to pitches of long duration; its meaning is unclear, but its musical context implies a sustained trill lasting the entire value of the note. Perhaps it is a trill which gradually increases in speed and number of oscillations, such as that described in François David's *Méthode nouvelle ou principes généraux pour apprendre facilement la musique et l'art de chanter* (Paris, 1737).[43] The symbols + and ⌣ appear in non-autograph sources and probably indicate nothing more extensive than a short trill.

Among the expressive rhythmic liberties practiced in seventeenth-century France was *inégalité*, or inequality. This was a convention, generally unwritten, of performing certain stepwise successions of evenly notated pitches in an uneven rhythm, either short-long or (more often) long-short. A passage of music notated in evenly written notes would thereby receive an agogic accent on the rhythmically extended note of the pair. *Inégalité* is most certainly called for in the slurred eighth-note passages of Orpheus's violin solo (mm. 58–88) from *Orphée descendant aux enfers*. Other rhythmic alterations the knowledgeable performer may wish to apply to the preludes, airs, and ensembles of *Orphée descendant aux enfers* are: (1) the performance of groups of short upbeat notes *(tirades)*, played more rapidly than as written; (2) the performance practice of double dotting notes and rests; and (3) the rhythmic synchronization of all parts (instrumental and vocal).[44]

Indications of dynamics are scarce in the sources, though the words *echo* and *piano* furnish occasional guidelines for performance. However, dynamic gradations should be applied to various passages, and a close inspection of the musical texture, instrumentation, and text will aid the performer in finding suitable dynamic levels throughout. As a general rule, *crescendi* and *diminuendi* should be minimized; rather, any change in dynamic level should be "terraced."

For passages or sections in which there is a change of meter, suggested tempo relationships have been supplied in the form of note equations (e.g., $\mathord{\downarrow} = \mathord{\downarrow}\cdot$). These editorial indications are arrived at through the application of the tempo and proportional implications inherent in baroque meters, and through careful consideration of the sung texts and musical structures. In no way should the editorial recommendations be interpreted in a rigid or inflexible manner, particularly when performing recitative. Rather, the performer must be guided by the meaning and spirit of the words and vary the tempo accordingly within the general framework of these tempo relationships.

Critical Notes

Variants in the manuscripts are logged against the present edition and reported in the Critical Notes. Readings in which the primary source differs from the edition are readings in which the primary source has been emended.

The following abbreviations are used: F-Pn = Bibliothèque Nationale, Paris; F-AB = Bibliothèque Municipale, Musée Calvet, Avignon; M = measure; BDs = *basdessus*; BC = *basse continüe*; BTa = *basse-taille*; C = *canto*; DmDs = *demi-dessus*; Ds = *dessus*; Flab = *flûte à bec*; FlAl = *flûte allemande*; HCn = *haute-contre*; HTa = *haute-taille*; Vle = *viole*; Vn = *viollon*; VnOr = *viollon d'Orphée*. Divisi parts are distinguished by arabic numerals, e.g., Vn 1. Pitches are indicated in accordance with the Helmholtz system, wherein c' = middle C, c" = the C above middle C, and so forth. Unless identified otherwise in the comments, the source of variant readings is the primary source.

Orphée descendant aux enfers

Autograph MS: F-Pn, Rés. Vm¹ 259, VI, fols. 11–16

Mm. 1–2, VnOr, source shows inscription "Orphee" above staff. M. 5, VnOr, symbol ♪ in source transcribed here as eighth-rest; is apparently equivalent to source symbol ↑ transcribed as eighth-rest in m. 10, FlAl, as confirmed by imitation between the parts. M. 13, source shows inscriptions "viollon" beside top staff, "viollon" beside second staff, and "flutes" beside third staff. M. 15, source shows inscription "fl al et abec" below third staff. M. 21, source shows inscriptions "abec" beside upper note, and "all." beside lower note of third staff. M. 96, all parts, m. ends with a single barline. M. 99, source shows inscriptions "vion" below top staff and below second staff. Mm. 110–11, source shows inscriptions "fl seules" above system, "fl abec" above top staff, and "fl seule" above second staff. Mm. 125–26, source shows inscriptions "viol seul" above top staff and "vio seul" below second staff. M. 127, all parts, repeat of mm. 98–127 is written out. Mm. 128–29, source shows inscriptions "fl abec et vio" above top staff and "fl et vio" above second staff. M. 130, source shows inscriptions "vio" above second staff and "fl" below second staff. M. 132, source shows inscriptions "vio" above top staff and "fl" below top staff. M. 134, source shows inscriptions "vs" above top staff and "vs" below top staff. M. 136, source shows inscriptions "fls" above second staff and "fls" below second staff. M. 137, source shows inscription "vions" above top staff. M. 148, source shows inscriptions "vions" beside top staff and "fls" beside second staff. M.

175, Orphée, source has "des" instead of "ou." M. 197, all parts, source indication "naturel" appearing above the system indicates the cancellation of the sharp from the previous system; source shows sharps rubbed out at the beginning of the system. Mm. 210–12, Tantale, last text word in section is "resveille." M. 227, source shows inscriptions "vions" beside top staff and "fl." beside second staff. Mm. 258–59, source shows inscriptions "pʳ dessus" below top staff and "sᵈ dessus" above top staff. M. 283, source shows inscriptions "vions" beside top staff, and "fls" beside second staff; m. ends with single barline in all parts. Mm. 299–373, all parts, source notation is in *croches blanches*. M. 311, source shows inscriptions "vions" beside top staff and "fls" beside second staff. M. 344, source shows inscriptions "v et fl ab" above top staff and "v et fl dal" below top staff. M. 360, source shows inscriptions "fls et vs" both above and below top staff. M. 363, source shows inscriptions "v et fl ab" beside top staff and "v et fl dal" beside second staff. M. 373, all parts, source shows inscription "fin" and a measure-count number, "400" (which counts the written-out repeat of mm. 98–127), to the right of the double barline.

Cantate françoise de M. Charpentier

F-AB, MS 1182, pp. 25–32

Second Dessus is labeled "Second Dessuse." M. 17, note 2–m. 28, note 1, BC, bass line misaligned relative to other parts—probably a copying error, since m. 27 (an empty m.) is crossed out, and thereafter the bass line appears to be correctly aligned. M. 28, BC, note 1 is e.

Serenata a tre voci e simphonia

Autograph MS: F-Pn, Rés. Vm¹ 259, VII, fols. 18–24ᵛ

M. 57, Vn 1, beats 1 and 2, half-rest; custos at end of previous m. indicates d". M. 62, BC, note 2, bass figure is ♭⁶₄. M. 96, HCn, extra syllable of text ("-ti") underlaid to note 1. M. 141, beat 2–m. 143, beat 1¹/₂, Vn 2, source shows rubbed-out passage comprised of imitative entry of Vn 1 line beginning with beat 4 of m. 141. M. 152, all parts, word "Suitte" written above Vn 1 in a blank staff separating the two systems. M. 159, note 5–m. 160, BTa, text is "contenton." M. 182, Vn 2, rest is a quarter-rest. M. 190, BC, a measure-count number, "190," appears to the right of the double barline.

Superbo amore

F-Pn, Vm⁷ 18, pp. 70–72

M. 1, all parts, source shows inscription "di Charpentiers" above the system. M. 16, all parts, source shows inscription "seguita" above the system. M. 39, BC, source shows bass figures "4 3" placed above BC line and crossed out.

Il mondo così và

F-Pn, Vm⁷ 18, pp. 70–72

M. 1, all parts, source shows inscription "di Char." to the left of the system. M. 8, BC, note 1 has bass figure "4" above it. M. 14, all parts, source lacks barline at end of m. M. 16, all parts, source shows inscription "seguita" to the left of the system.

Beate mie pene

TRANSCRIPTION SOURCE
F-Pn, Vm⁷ 53, pp. 74–77 (hereafter source A)

CONCORDANCE
F-Pn, Vm⁷ 8, fols. 17–20 (hereafter source B)

M. 1 and throughout, all parts, notation is in *croches blanches* in both sources. M. 1, source A shows inscription "a 2ᵉ Del Sʳ. Charpentier" above the system. Title page, source B shows inscription "Beate mie Pené / Duo a doi canti de / Sign. / Charpentier"; m. 1, BC, source B shows inscription "Aria del Sign Charpentier a doi canti / Basso continuo" above the staff; m. 1, C1, source B shows inscription "aria a doi canti del Sign. Charpentier. Canto 1ᵒ" above the staff; m. 1, C2, source B shows inscription "Aria a doi canti del Sign. Charpentier Canto 2ᵒ." above the staff. Mm. 1–3, BC, text "Beate catene" under BC line in source B. M. 17, C1, note 2 is quarter-rest and white eighth-note in source B; C2, note 3 is quarter-rest and white eighth-note in source B. M. 20, C2, note 3 is white eighth-note (e″) in source A. M. 29–m. 30, note 1, BC, no tie in source A. M. 33, C2, note 3 is c″ in source A; corrected here by analogy with source B. M. 39, note 5–m. 40, note 2, C2, no tie or slur in source A. M. 42, BC, note 1 is g, figured with a flat, in source B. M. 48, C2, notes 1 and 2 are dotted half-note and white eighth-note in source B. M. 61, C1, note 2 is c″ in source B. M. 62–m. 63, note 1, BC, no tie in source A. M. 68, C2, notes 1–3 are half-note (b′-flat), dotted white eighth-note (b′-flat), white sixteenth-note (b′-flat) in source B. M. 70, C1, source B has half-note (f″), dotted white eighth-note (f″), white sixteenth-note (f″), half-note (e″); C2, note 3 is obscured in the binding of source B. M. 72, C1, notes 1–3, source B has half-note (g′), half-note (a′), dotted white eighth-note (a′), white sixteenth-note (b′); C2, notes 1–3, source B has half-note (b′-flat), half-note (c″), dotted white eighth-note (c″), white sixteenth-note (d″). Mm. 73–75, C1, text reads, "-mor non gode in a-" in source B. M. 74, C1, notes 1–2, source B has half-note (d″), white eighth-note (d″), white eighth-note (e″); note 3 is f″-natural in source A and is corrected by analogy with source B. M. 76, C1, source B has half-note (e″) and dotted white eighth-note (e″), with remainder of line obscured in the binding. M. 76, C2, notes 1–2, source B has half-note (d″), white eighth-note (d″), white eighth-note (d″). Mm. 78–79, C2, source B has repeat signs with "litchi cantene" written below "Be-ate mie pene fe-." M. 95, BC, no slur between notes 1 and 2 in source A. M. 98, C1, notes 1–2, source B has half-note (f″), dotted white eighth-note (f″), white sixteenth-note (f″). M. 100, C2, notes 1–2, source B has half-note (c″), dotted white eighth-note (c″), white sixteenth-note (c″). M. 102, C1, notes 1–2, source B has half-note (g″), dotted white eighth-note (g″), white sixteenth-note (g″). M. 104, C1, notes 1–2, source B has half-note (e″), dotted white eighth-note (e″), white sixteenth-note (e″); C2, notes 2–3 obscured in the binding of source B. M. 108, C1, notes 1–2, source B has half-note (g′), dotted white eighth-note (g′), white sixteenth-note (a′). M. 112, C2, notes 1–2, source B has half-note (g′), dotted white eighth-note (g″), white sixteenth-note (g′), note 3 obscured in the binding of source B. Mm. 113–15, C1, source B has repeat signs; repeat written out here in mm. 115–17. M. 114, C1, notes 1–2, source B has half-note (g′), dotted white eighth-note (g′), white sixteenth-note (g′); notes 1–2, text in source B is "gaude." Mm. 113–17, C2, text in source B is "non god' in amor," with the elision not spelled out rhythmically. M. 115, all parts, source A has no *piano* indication; added by analogy with C2 part in source B; note 1 is a dotted whole-note and ends the piece in source A.

Epitaphium Carpentarij

Autograph MS, except for first folio; F-Pn, Rés. Vm¹ 259, XIII, fols. 60ᵛ–65

Mm. 1–20, all parts, first folio of source is written in a different (and apparently later) hand. Whereas the following folios show staves spaced equidistantly, the staves of the first folio are grouped in systems of four; the vocal music begins on a staff drawn above the top staff of the third system, bearing at the left side the inscription "Ignatius." At the bottom of the folio appear the inscriptions "Suivez à laise" and "Umbra." M. 10, Ignatius, notes 2–3 are eighth-note tied to quarter-note. M. 20, source shows inscription "umbra" below system. Mm. 32–33, BC, notes written as three black whole-notes with barline intersecting note 2 of m. 32. Mm. 50–69, all parts, source notation is in *croches blanches*. M. 70–m. 71, note 1, BC line cut off at bottom of fol. 61; custos (at end of previous system in source) indicates the pitch F. Mm. 134–255, all parts, source notation is in *croches blanches*. M. 163, source shows inscriptions "le mesme" to the left of the three vocal staves. Mm. 226–27, BC line cut off at bottom of fol. 62ᵛ. M. 232, BC, figures partially cut off at bottom of fol. 62ᵛ. Mm. 256 and 271, all parts, these mm. end with a single barline. M. 257, Marcellus and BC, inscription "naturel" (indicating cancellation of sharps from the previous key signature) appears above vocal staff and to the left of BC staff. M. 275, note 1, BC line partially cut off at bottom of fol. 63. Mm. 279–99, all parts, source notation is in *croches blanches*. M. 334, BC, figures partially cut off at bottom of fol. 63ᵛ. M. 352, BC, figures are $^{9\,7}_{\,6}$. Mm. 354–61, all parts, source notation is in *croches blanches*. M. 391, BC, measure-count number, "391," appears below BC line.

Acknowledgments

I wish to express my gratitude to H. Wiley Hitchcock, who alerted me to the existence of these interesting works, and to the Bibliothèque Nationale, Paris, and the Bibliothèque Municipale, Musée Calvet, in Avignon for supplying reproductions of the manuscripts. For his help with the Italian translations, I am indebted to Denis Stevens. The transcription and translation of the Latin text was entirely the work of Professor Jo-Ann Shelton of the Department of Classics at the University of California, Santa Barbara. I also wish to show my appreciation to the many others who have given me advice and encouragement with this project.

John S. Powell

Notes

1. H.W. Hitchcock, *Les oeuvres de Marc-Antoine Charpentier: Catalogue raisonné* (Paris: Picard, 1982), pp. 15–22. In the course of this Preface, discussions of works by Charpentier include, where appropriate, citation-numbers (expressed as, e.g., "H. 471") used to identify these works in Hitchcock's *Catalogue raisonné*.

2. These are the two main types of cantata distinguished in the Italian repertory of the seventeenth and early eighteenth centuries. They are described by Eleanor Caluori as *ariette corte* (short ariettas) and *arie di più parti* (arias in several sections) in *The Cantatas of Luigi Rossi: Analysis and Thematic Index* (Ann Arbor: UMI Research Press, 1981), 2 vols.

3. The most important contemporary accounts of Charpentier's life appear in Sébastien de Brossard, *Catalogue des livres de musique . . . 1724* (F-Pn, Rés. Vm⁸ 21); Titon du Tillet, *Description du Parnasse françois* (Paris: Jean-Baptiste Coignard, 1727); and Titon du Tillet, *Le Parnasse françois* (Paris: Jean-Baptiste Coignard, 1727). Modern biographies include: Hitchcock, *Catalogue raisonné*, pp. 15–22; *Dictionnaire de musique*, s.v. "Charpentier, Marc-Antoine," by Guy-Lambert; Robert W. Lowe, *Marc-Antoine Charpentier et l'opéra de collège* (Paris: G. P. Maisonneuve & Larose, 1966); Eugene Borrel, "La vie musicale de M.-A. Charpentier d'après le Mercure Galant (1678–1704)," *XVIIᵉ siècle*, nos. 21–22 (1954): 433–41; *Die Musik in Geschichte und Gegenwart*, s.v. "Charpentier, Marc-Antoine," by Denise Launay; Claude Crussard, *Un musicien français oublié: Marc-Antoine Charpentier, 1634–1704* (Paris: Floury, 1945).

4. Sébastien de Brossard states, "Mʳ Charpentier, à ce que je crois Parisien" (*Catalogue*, p. 224), while Titon du Tillet, *Description*, p. 144, states in his entry on Charpentier, "Parisien." The daybook of the Sainte-Chapelle refers to the composer as a "natif du diocèse de Paris" (quoted in Michel Brenet, *Les musiciens de la Sainte-Chapelle du Palais* [Paris: Picard, 1910], p. 260).

5. The most complete discussion of this issue appears in Hitchcock, *Catalogue raisonné*, pp. 15–16.

6. For three years, according to the *Mercure galant* (February 1681), pp. 249–50.

7. It is not known whether Charpentier actually attended the Collegium Germanicum or served as one of its musicians, but he was familiar with at least one of Carissimi's oratorios, *Jephte*, of which the Bibliothèque Nationale owns a manuscript copied in Charpentier's hand (Vm¹ 1477).

8. See *The New Grove Dictionary of Music and Musicians*, s.v. "Dassoucy, Charles," by Margaret M. McGowan, for details pertaining to Dassoucy's life and career. Dassoucy obliquely refers to having known Charpentier in Rome in his *Rimes redoublées* (Paris: C. Nkgo, [1672]), p. 120; this passage is cited in Georges Mongrédièn, *Recueil des textes des documents du XVIIᵉ siècle relatifs à Molière* (Paris: Éditions du Centre National de la Recherche Scientifique, 1965), 1:400, and in Hitchcock, *Catalogue raisonné*, pp. 15–16, n. 6.

9. Sébastien de Brossard (*Catalogue*), in his biography on Charpentier, p. 224, writes, "À son retour d'Italie il travailla pendant quelque temps pour les comédiens français." On the other hand, Titon du Tillet (*Le Parnasse françois*, p. 490) states, "Etant de retour à Paris, Mademoiselle de Guise lui donna un appartement dans son Hôtel" (Upon returning to Paris, Mademoiselle de Guise gave him an apartment in her mansion).

10. *Mercure galant* (March 1688), p. 321. "Cette Musique estoit si bonne qu'on peut dire que celle de plusieurs grands Souverains n'en approche pas."

11. Thirteen of her musicians, including Charpentier, were granted individual bequests in a codicil to her will; see Lionel de La Laurencie, "Un opéra inédit de M.-A. Charpentier: *La descente d'Orphée aux enfers*," *Revue de musicologie* 10 (1929): 185–86.

12. Charpentier's name (abbreviated "Charp") appears next to *haute-contre* parts along with names of other singers in the service of the Duchesse de Guise in the following works: "Litanies de la vierge à 6 voix et deux dessus de violes" (H. 83); "Psalm David 50ᵐᵘˢ / Miserere des Jésuites" (H. 193); "Chant joyeux du temps de Pâques" (H. 339); "Nuptiae sacrae" (H. 412); "Caecilia virgo et martyr" (H. 413 and H. 415); "Sur la naissance de N. S. J. C. pastorale" (H. 482, H. 483, and H. 483a); "Il faut rire et chanter: dispute de bergers" (H. 484); "La couronne de fleurs: pastorale" (H. 486); "Les arts florissants: opéra" (H. 487); and "La descente d'Orphée aux enfers" (H. 488).

13. *Le registre de La Grange, 1659–1685*, ed. Bert Edward Young and Grace Philputt Young (Paris: E. Droz, 1947), 1:137, informs us for 8 July 1672:

> Nᵃ encores que le Mariage forcé qui a esté joué auec la Comtesse d'Escarbagnas a esté accompagné d'ornemens dont Monsr Charpentier a faict la Musique, et Monsr de Beauchamps les balletz, M. Baraillon les habitz, et M. de Villiers auoit employ dans la musique des Intermedes.
>
> (Again, note that *The Forced Marriage*, which played with *The Countess of Escarbagnas*, was accompanied with embellishments—for which Monsieur Charpentier created the music, Monsieur de Beauchamps the dances, M. Baraillon the costumes, and M. de Villiers was used in the vocal music of the interludes.)

Charpentier may have played violin in the orchestra for the premiere of *Psyché* (1671) and later for *Le ballet des ballets* (1672), which would have brought him into contact with Molière; the *livrets* for these entertainments contained in the Bibliothèque Nationale (Thᴮ 2078 and Thᴮ 2392) list a Charpentier among the violinists performing the "Air pour les Polichinelles & les Matassins" of the *Entrée de la suite de Mome*, but whether or not this Charpentier was Marc-Antoine remains unknown. (Hitchcock, *Catalogue raisonné*, p. 16, n. 11, lists a number of musicians active in Paris at this time with the surname Charpentier.)

14. This 1672 version of *Le mariage forcé* will be published by A-R Editions, Inc., in a forthcoming volume entitled: *Marc-Antoine Charpentier: Music for Molière's Comedies*, ed. John S. Powell.

15. For a survey of this aspect of Charpentier's career, see H. Wiley Hitchcock, "Marc-Antoine Charpentier and the Comédie-Française," *Journal of the American Musicological Society* 24 (1971): 255–81.

16. *Mercure galant* (March 1681), p. 306:

> En arrivant à Saint-Cloud, le Roi congédia toute sa musique et voulut **entendre celle de Mᵍʳ le Dauphin** jusqu'à son retour à Saint-Germain. Elle a tous les jours chanté à la messe des motets de M. Charpentier, et Sa Majesté n'en a point voulu entendre d'autres, quoiqu'on lui en eût proposé.

17. The *Mercure galant* (April 1683), pp. 310–15, gives an account of this competition; reprinted in Hitchcock, *Catalogue raisonné*, p. 19.

18. The *Mercure galant* (June 1683), pp. 267–68, states:

> J'ai à vous apprendre en vous parlant de musique que le Roi un peu avant son départ donna un pension à Mʳ Charpentier. Vous savez qu'il a toujours composé la musique qu'on a chantée à la Messe de Monseigneur le Dauphin, lors que ce prince n'assistait pas à celle du Roi.
>
> (I have to inform you, speaking of music, that the King just before his departure gave a pension to Monsieur Charpentier. You know that he has always composed the music sung at the Mass of Monseigneur the Dauphin when this prince did not attend that of the King.)

19. See Michel Brenet, *Les musiciens de la Sainte-Chapelle du Palais* (Paris: Picard, 1910), which documents Charpentier's years at the Sainte-Chapelle.

20. One work from this category that is not included in this edition is *Epithalamio in lode dell'altezza serenissima elettorale di Massimiliano Emanuel duca di Baviera* (H. 473); this cantata is transcribed in James P. Dunn, "The *Grands Motets* of Marc-Antoine Charpentier" (Ph.D. diss., University of Iowa, 1962), 2:67–92. See also Henri Quittard, "Note sur un ouvrage inédit de Marc-Antoine Charpentier," *Zeitschrift der internationalen Musikgesellschaft* 6 (1905): 323–30.

21. These perimeters are determined from the earliest and latest Charpentier works to which we can affix a definite date: the *Ouver-*

ture de la Comtesse d'Escarbagnas and *Intermèdes nouveaux du Mariage forcé* (H. 494, performed 8 July 1672); and his dramatic motet *Judicium Salomonis* (H. 422, 1702).

22. This work is discussed, and excerpts from it transcribed, in the following sources: Henri Quittard, "Orphée descendant aux enfers," *Tablettes de la schola* 6 (15 January 1904): 3–4; Idem, "Orphée descendant aux enfers. Cantate française de Marc-Antoine Charpentier (1634–1704)," *Revue d'histoire et de critiques musicales* 9 (1904): 495–96 and 136–40; James R. Anthony, *French Baroque Music*, rev. ed. (New York: Norton, 1978), pp. 360–61; and David E. Tunley, *The Eighteenth-Century French Cantata* (London: Dennis Dobson, 1974), pp. 46–49.

23. Hitchcock presumably chose this date because of the proximity of other works in the same *cahier* of the composer's autographs which are known to have been written in 1683 (such as *Luctus de morte augustissimae Mariae Theresiae reginae Galliae*, H. 331). Henri Quittard ("Orphée descendant aux enfers," p. 495), however, also states that "certains indices, tirés du manuscrit, permettent cependant d'en fixer la composition aux environs de l'an 1683," although he doesn't mention what these "certains indices" are.

24. Lionel de La Laurencie, "Un opéra inédit de M.-A. Charpentier: *La descente d'Orphée aux enfers*," *Revue de musicologie* 10 (1929): 184, confirms Quittard's assertion ("Orphée descendant aux enfers," p. 495) that *Orphée descendant aux enfers* was intended for the private concerts of the Duchesse de Guise; this hypothesis has also been accepted by Anthony (*French Baroque Music*, p. 360).

25. Quittard, "Orphée descendant aux enfers," p. 495; Charpentier is known to have sung *haute-contre* in a number of works performed by the musical entourage of the Duchesse de Guise (see n. 12). The inscription "Orphee" above the first two measures of the "Viollon d'Orph[ée]" in the *Prélude* provides evidence that this instrumental part was played by the same musician who sang the role of Orpheus; see Plate I.

26. Crussard, *Un musicien français oublié*, p. 18, and Quittard, "Orphée descendant aux enfers," p. 495, both speculate that the work is incomplete; this hypothesis is given as fact in Gene E. Vollen, *The French Cantata: A Survey and Thematic Catalog* (Ann Arbor: UMI Research Press, 1982), pp. 395–96.

27. The opera *La descente d'Orphée aux enfers* (H. 488) was written for the Duchesse de Guise, and only the first two acts are extant. Among the characters in the opera appear Orphée (*haute-contre*, sung by Antheaume), Ixion (*haute-contre*, sung by Charpentier), and Tantale (tenor, sung by Bossan), which correspond to the characters in the dramatic cantata *Orphée descendant aux enfers*. It would be interesting to know which came first, the cantata or the opera.

28. Amadée Gastoué, "Notes sur les manuscrit et sur quelques oeuvres de M.-A. Charpentier," in *Mélanges de musicologie offerts à M. Lionel de La Laurencie* (Paris: E. Droz, 1933), p. 161, first called attention to this cantata, and transcribed the opening thirty-five measures (pp. 162–64). Manfred Bukofzer, *Music in the Baroque Era* (New York: Norton, 1947), p. 162, included the *Cantate françoise de M. Charpentier* in his discussion of Charpentier's cantatas: "His cantata 'Coulez' for solo voice and three instruments, written in the pathetic style of a plaintive pastoral, discloses how he adapted a noble bel-canto melody to the French style by the use of the French type of embellishments." Robert W. Lowe, *Marc-Antoine Charpentier et l'opéra de collège* (Paris: G.-P. Maisonneuve & Larose, 1966), p. 14, also accepted its authenticity, and speculated that the existence of this manuscript in Avignon may indicate that Charpentier stayed there for a time en route from Rome to Paris. Anthony (*French Baroque Music*, p. 360) holds a less exalted opinion of this cantata, and states, "It is a short fragment of little musical interest for solo voice (tenor), two violins and continuo." Musical interest aside, *Cantate françoise de M. Charpentier* does not appear to be a fragment in the sense of being incomplete: the text follows an A-B-A scheme which receives a through-composed musical setting, and there is no indication of any missing music at either the beginning or the end. Vollen (*The French Cantata*, p. 396) includes this work among Charpentier's cantatas in his thematic catalog, where he inexplicably notates the vocal incipit with the bass clef.

29. Hitchcock, *Catalogue raisonné*, p. 346.

30. James R. Anthony, "A Source for Secular Vocal Music in 18th-Century Avignon: MS 1182 of the Bibliothèque du Museum Calvet," *Acta musicologica* 54 (January–December 1982): 267–69.

31. Anthony, *French Baroque Music*, p. 360.

32. Anthony, "A Source for Secular Vocal Music," p. 269.

33. Arias that begin with a preliminary statement of the initial melodic motif, first sung and then echoed by the instruments, occur occasionally in the cantatas of Rossi and became established later in the cantatas and operas of Legrenzi and Cesti.

34. Regarding the French style characteristics of *Cantate françoise de M. Charpentier*, Anthony ("A Source for Secular Vocal Music," p. 268) writes:

> On the other hand, "Coulez, coulez" clearly exhibits the particularly French stylistic features of those nature scenes or "sommeils" found alike in 17th- and 18th-century French stage music and cantata. To wit: the voice part is characterized by a narrow range, basically conjunct motion and a generally syllabic treatment of the text with a cliché melisma on such a word as "coulez"; the writing for the two violins is extremely conservative and predominately note against note; there is a limited use of discreet chromaticism, and the rhythmic figure of dotted quarter and eighth appears frequently.

35. The spelling *simphonia* given in the source is apparently a hybrid of the Italian *sinfonia* and the French *simphonie*.

36. Hitchcock, *Catalogue raisonné*, p. 342.

37. ". . . elle est distincte de la Sérénade pour le Sicilien," Gastoué, "Notes sur les manuscrits," pp. 157–58. In his entry for *Sérénade pour Le Sicilien* (H. 497), Hitchcock speculates that "the music was probably composed for a revival of the play which opened in Paris on 9 June 1679" (p. 372), but he is undoubtedly in error. A volume contained in the Bibliothèque-Musée de la Comédie-Française (F-Pcf) entitled *Recüeil complet de vaudevilles et airs choisis qui ont eté chantés à la Comédie-Française depuis l'année 1659* (Paris: aux adresses ordinaires, 1759) includes just the vocal parts (without *basse continüe*) under the heading "Air ajouté au Sicilien en 1695" (pp. 4–5); on 4 January 1695, *Le Sicilien* was revived as a *comédie-ballet* for a series of performances during January and February for which the account books list nine dancers, one paid singer (along with the actor/singer de Villiers, who was in the cast), two costumes (presumably for the singers), and a harpsichord (*Archives de la Comédie-Française [Petit Registre]*, 4 January–14 February 1695, under date of 4 January 1695). Certainly it was for the 1695 run that Charpentier provided these new musical *intermèdes*, which are included in this author's volume, *Marc-Antoine Charpentier: Music for Molière's Comedies* (A-R Editions: Madison, Wis., forthcoming).

38. Before his tenure at the Sainte-Chapelle du Palais, François Chaperon taught at the choir school of Saint-Germain l'Auxerrois, where among his students was the young Marin Marais (see John Hsu, ed., *Marin Marais: The Instrumental Works* [New York: Broude Brothers, 1980], vol. 1, *Pieces à une et à deux violes*, p. xiii) and Michel Richard Delalande (Titon du Tillet, *Le Parnasse françois*, p. 612). On 4 October 1679 he succeeded René Ouvrard as *maître de musique* at the Sainte-Chapelle. Among his young charges was Michel L'Affilard, who later became a composer of court airs and the author of *Principes très faciles pour apprendre la musique* (Paris, 1694; reprinted 1697, 1702, 1705, 1710, and 1717). The *Mercure de France* (June 1738, p. 1733) also credits Chaperon as being the teacher of Jean-François Lalouette and Pascal Collasse and refers to him as "the most learned musician of his time" (cited in Brenet, *Les musiciens de la Sainte-Chapelle du Palais*, p. 260n). In April of 1680 Chaperon initiated the "musiques extraordinaires" for the Tenebrae services at the Sainte-Chapelle, at which crowds gathered to hear music by Chaperon and his students; the *Mercure galant* (April 1680, p. 324) informs us that "on a couru en foule à la Sainte-Chapelle et a l'Abbaye-aux-Bois. Ce qu'on entendit à la Sainte-Chapelle était de Mrs Chaperon, La Lande et Lalouëte et à l'Abbaye-aux-Bois de Mr Charpentier" (everyone rushes to the Sainte-Chapelle and to the Abbaye-aux-Bois. The music heard at the Sainte-Chapelle is by Chaperon, La Lande [Delalande], and Lalouette, and that at the Abbaye-aux-Bois is by Charpentier). On 21 April 1683 Chaperon was made a "clerc ordinaire," and served in this capacity as *maître de musique* until his death on 20 May 1698. For documentation of Chaperon's years at the Sainte-Chapelle, see Brenet, *Les musiciens de la Sainte-Chapelle du Palais*.

39. Here and elsewhere, puns on the names Carissimi (*cara* = dear; *carissimi* = dearest) and Chaperon (*caprinus* = goatish or goat-like) are numerous.

40. Regarding the manuscript source of *Epitaphium Carpentarij*

(F-Pn, Vm¹ 259, XIII, fols. 60ᵛ–65), Hitchcock (*Catalogue raisonné*, pp. 35–36) makes the following observations:

> Cahier (a) follows cahiers "I" and "II" in volume XIII of the "Mélanges" and completes it. Its original outer double leaf has been replaced by one of different paper. On the verso of the first leaf (60ᵛ) is written the opening of the peculiar and punningly humorous Latin cantata *Epitaphium Carpentarij* (Cat. 474), in which thinly disguised jibes are made at François Chaperon (Charpentier's predecessor at the Sainte-Chapelle) and his "musica capronia" (goatish music). Alone among the thousands of pages in the "Mélanges," this page is written in a copyist's hand (although the pages containing the remainder of the work, 61–65, are in Charpentier's). Clearly, the original double sheet enclosing the cahier—its first page bearing in all probability a cahier number—was removed, replaced by a different enclosing double sheet, and the beginning of the cantata recopied, thus preserving the entire work. The musical style, like that of the only other composition in the cahier, a setting of the *Stabat Mater* sequence (Cat. 15), is mature but cannot be pin-pointed in time: we leave the dating of the cahier as "unknown."

41. The libelous and punning nature of *Epitaphium Carpentarij* suggests that it was intended for a select audience—such as that which attended performances of Charpentier's oratorios at the Collège Louis-le-Grand, on rue Saint-Jacques, or at the Jesuit "Maison Professe," on rue Saint-Antoine. Other textual evidence that supports this hypothesis includes: (1) the text, which is entirely in Latin; (2) the parodic religious nature of many passages (e.g., "Beatus ille qui pro delendis culpis suis fastidiosa et discordi caproni musica aures suas fatigabit, castigabit, capronabit . . ."); and (3) the minor character Ignatius, presumably named after the founder of the Jesuit order, Ignatius of Loyola (1492–1556).

42. According to Crussard (*Un musicien français oublié: Marc-Antoine Charpentier, 1634–1704*, p. 16), the musical forces at the Maison de Guise consisted "de huit ou dix chanteurs, d'un clavecin et d'une basse de viole pour le *continuo* auxquels s'adjoignaient, pour les sinfonies deux uniques dessus de viole" (of eight or ten singers, a harpsichord and a bass viol for the continuo, to which would be added two single treble viols for the sinfonias).

43. See James R. Anthony, ed., *De profundis by Michel-Richard Delalande* (Chapel Hill, 1980), pp. 16–17.

44. For further guidance in baroque performance practice, see Robert Donington's *Baroque Music: Style and Performance* (New York: Norton, 1982).

Texts and Translations

Orphée descendant aux enfers

I. Prélude

II. Récit d'Orphée [sur le viollon]

III. Air d'Orphée

ORPHÉE:
Effroyables enfers où je conduis mes pas,
aucun de vos tourmens n'esgalle mon supplice.
Hélas! Ou rendez moy mon aymable Euridice
ou laissez moy descendre aux ombres du trépas.

IV. Duo

TANTALE:
Quelle douce harmonie a frappé mon oreille
et de tous mes tourmens a calmé la rigueur?

TANTALE ET IXION:
D'où vient que je soupire et qu'au fond de mon coeur
de mes jeunes amours la flamme se réveille?

V. Air

ORPHÉE:
Vos plus grands criminels, rongés par des vautours
sur leurs tristes rochers, endurent moins de peine
qu'un malheureux amant que la mort inhumaine
sépare pour jamais de ses tendres amours.

VI. Duo et Trio

TANTALE ET IXION:
Ne cherchons plus d'où vient cette tendresse
qui remplit notre coeur d'une douce allégresse;
l'amour dont le divin flambeau
esclaire cet amant dans la nuit du tombeau
nous a frappéz d'un rayon de sa flamme.

ORPHEUS, TATALUS, AND IXION:
Hélas! Rien n'est égal au bonheur des amans,
pour peu que l'amour touche une âme

elle ne ressent $\left\{\begin{array}{l}\text{point}\\\text{plus}\end{array}\right\}$ tous les autres tourmens.

Cantate françoise de M. Charpentier

Couléz, couléz charmans ruisseaux,
   portés par tout ma triste plainte.
Pour fuir l'amour, le bruit et la contrainte,
   j'estois venû dans ce hameau;
   je n'aimois rien que mon troupeau,
j'estois heureuz, quand la cruelle Aminte
   m'engagea dans un lien nouveau.
   J'ay découvert un feu si beau,

Orpheus Descends into the Underworld

I. Prelude

II. Solo of Orpheus on the Violin

III. Air of Orpheus

ORPHEUS:
Frightful underworld to where I journey,
none of your torments can match my anguish.
Alas! Return to me my beloved Eurydice
or let me descend into the shades of death.

IV. Duo

TANTALUS:
What sweet harmony has struck my ear
and has eased the harshness of my torments?

TANTALUS AND IXION:
How is it that I sigh, and from the depths of my heart
the flame of my youthful loves is reawakened?

V. Air

ORPHEUS:
Your greatest criminals, gnawed upon by vultures
on their gloomy rocks suffer less pain
than an ill-starred lover whom heartless death
forever separates from his tender loves.

VI. Duet and Trio

TANTALUS AND IXION:
Let us no longer seek from whence comes this tenderness
that fills our heart with sweet joyfulness:
Love, whose divine torch
lights this lover in the darkness of the tomb,
has struck us with a ray from its flame.

ORPHÉE, TANTALE, ET IXION:
Alas! Nothing can equal the good fortune of lovers
for however slightly love touches a soul,

the soul $\left\{\begin{array}{l}\text{does not feel}\\\text{no longer feels}\end{array}\right\}$ all of the other torments.

French Cantata by M. Charpentier

Flow, flow, charming brooklets,
   carry everywhere my sad lament.
To flee from love—its tumult and bonds—
   I came to this hamlet;
   I loved nothing but my flock,
I was happy, until the cruel Amynta
   involved me in a new bond.
   I discovered a fire so lovely,

mais toujours dans $\begin{Bmatrix} \text{ses yeux} \\ \text{mon coeur} \end{Bmatrix}$ la froideur
est dépeinte.
    Couléz, couléz charmans ruisseaux,
    portés par tout ma triste plainte.

but coldness is forever painted in $\begin{Bmatrix} \text{her eyes.} \\ \text{my heart.} \end{Bmatrix}$
    Flow, flow, charming brooklets,
    carry everywhere my sad lament.

Serenata a tre voci e simphonia

Sù sù sù, non dormite amanti,
ne vi stancate per lunghi pianti:
sospirate, piangete, ardete!
Vergognoso è il riposo:
Amor non vuole dormiglioso campion
ne le sue schole.

Io non dormo, io non riposo,
e s'il ciel già s'oscuró
cercando vó un più bel sole
entro due luci ascoso.

Io tra pene e tra sospiri
immortal serbo mia fè,
e sono a me premio sempre
bastante i miei martiri.

Il mio cuor, nobil guerriero,
nel periglio lieto stà;
ne bramar sà vanto o gloria
maggior del suo pensiero.

Se può dormir un core
lieto e contento
nel suo tormento,
nò nò nò, non sente amore;
e chi il riposo brama,
nò, che non arde,
nò, che non ama.

Serenade for Three Voices and Symphony

Rise up, do not sleep, lovers,
and don't tire of lengthy plaints:
sigh, weep, burn!
Repose is shameful:
Love does not want a sleepy champion
in his school.

I do not sleep, I do not rest,
and should the sky cloud over
I shall seek a more beautiful sun
hidden within two eyes.

I, among pains and among sighs
unending, keep my faith,
and my torments are always
enough of a reward for me.

My heart, noble warrior,
in danger remains cheerful;
and cannot desire glory or credit
greater than it can think of.

If a heart can sleep
joyful and content
in its torment,
no, no, no, it does not feel love;
and he who desires rest,
no, does not burn,
no, does not love.

Superbo amore

    Superbo amore,
    al mondo imperi,
    ma nel mio core
    regnar non speri:
    un nume infante
    d'alma regnante
non trionferà libertà!

Proud Love

    Proud love,
    you rule the world,
    but in my heart
    you cannot hope to reign:
    a child-god
    with a ruling soul
will not overcome liberty!

Il mondo così và

    Il mondo così và:
    dianzi gradito,
    hora schernito,
    provo strati e crudeltà.
Chi semina il gioir racoglie i pianti:
imparate a mie spese, ô folli amanti!
    Della femina a'l si
    pazzo è chi crede;
    costanza e fede
    dal suo cor donna sbandi.
Più non vi credonò, donne incostanti:
imparate a mie spese, ô folli amanti!

So Goes the World

    So goes the world:
    formerly welcome,
    now despised,
    I experience difficulties and harshness.
He who spreads joy gathers tears:
learn at my expense, O foolish lovers!
    He is mad
    who believes in the "yes" of a woman;
    for a lady banishes
    loyalty and trust from her heart.
They won't believe you anymore, inconstant women:
learn at my expense, O foolish lovers!

Beate mie pene

Beate mie pene,
felici catene,
legami del cor.
Deh, non mi lasciate,
a me diventate
più crudeli ôgn'hor;
chi non v'ha provate
non gode in amor.

Epitaphium Carpentarij

Interlocutores: Ignatius, Marcellus,
    Umbra Carpentarij, Tres angeli

IGNATIUS:
Quid audio, quod murmur horrisonum
simul es harmonicum aures meas pepulis?

MARCELLUS:
Quid video? Terra tremit.
Hic lapis inhiat.
Hic tumulus evomit umbram.
O portentum, fugiamus!

UMBRA:
Amici, viatores, nolite timere.
Sistite gradum et audite verba oris mei.
Hic terminus viae et vitae vestrae ac meae.
Ille ego qui natus pridem ac notus eram saeculo

endonatus hoc late o nudus nullusque sepulchro
pulvis, finis et esca vermium.
Satis vixi. Sed parum si spectetur aeternitas.

IG., MAR., UM.:
O aeternitas quam longa; o vita quaem brevis es.

UMBRA:
Musicus eram, inter bonos a bonis,

et inter ignaros ab ignaris nuncupatus.
Et cum multo major numerus esset eorum
qui me spernebant quam qui laudabant,
musica mihi parvus honos
sed magnum onus fuit; et, sicut
ego nihil nascens intuli in hunc mundum,
ita moriens nihil abstuli.

IG., MAR.:
Dic nobis, umbra chara,[1]
multumne differt caelestis a terrena musica.

UMBRA:
Ah socii, qui Carissimi nomen habebat in terris

Capronus, Chapronus vocatur in coelis.[2]
Domine, Deus meus, quem amo, quem possideo:
sana, purifica, sanctifica aures istorum

ut possint audire sacros angelorum concentus.
Audivit Deus deprecationem meam.
Tacete socii. Silete. Tacete.

Blessed Be My Sufferings

Blessed be my sufferings,
happy chains,
bonds of the heart.
Ah, leave me not to myself,
having become
always more cruel;
he who has not experienced it
does not take pleasure in love.

Funeral Oration of Charpentier

Speakers: Ignatius, Marcellus,
    Spirit of Charpentier, Three Angels

IGNATIUS:
What do I hear, what horrible-sounding roar,
yet similar to harmony, has struck my ears?

MARCELLUS:
What do I see? The earth trembles.
The rock gapes open.
The tomb disgorges a spirit!
Oh, a monster, let us flee!

SPIRIT:
Friends, travelers, do not be afraid.
Stop and listen to my words.
This is the end of the road of life—yours and mine.
I am he who was born long ago and had been known
    widely during this century,
but I am now naked and nothing, dust in a tomb,
an end, and the food of worms.
I have lived enough. But only briefly should all eter-
    nity be considered.

IG., MAR., SP.:
O eternity, how long you are; O life, how brief.

SPIRIT:
I was a musician, considered among the good musi-
    cians by the good,
and among the ignorant musicians by the ignorant.
And since more numerous were those
who scorned me than those who praised me,
music became a small honor
and a heavy burden; and just as
I, when born, brought nothing into this world,
thus, when dying, I took nothing away.

IG., MAR.:
Tell us, dear spirit,
whether heavenly music differs from earthly music.

SPIRIT:
Ah, comrades, he who held the name of Carissimi
    while on earth
is called Chaperon in heaven.
O Lord, my God, whom I love and cherish:
make healthy, purify, and sanctify the ears of these
    men,
so that they can hear the sacred concert of the angels.
God has heard my prayer.
Be silent, comrades. Be still. Be silent.

Trois anges:
Profitentes unitatem,
veneremur trinitatem
pari reverentia,
tres personas asserentes
personali differentes
a se differentia.

Patri natus est aequalis,
nec id tollit personalis
amborum distinctio;
patri compar filioque
spiritalis ab utroque
procedit connexio.

Pater, verbum, sanctum flamen,
Deus unus sed hi tamen
habent quaedam propria.

Una virtus, unum numen,
unus splendor, unum lumen,
una tribus gloria.

Ig., Mar., Um.:
O suave melos, o dulcis anticapronica musica.

Ig., Mar.:
Taedet me vitae meae. Ah quando, anima mea,
ad coelestem patriam volabis,
ut mellito hujus ce melodiae nectare replearis?

Umbra:
O amici, vivite laeti, at non immemores lethi.
Quis enim vestrum scit an cras an hodie
an hac ipsa forsitan hora sit moriendum.
Poenitentiam agite, ad caproni musicam currite.
Hanc in supplicium vobis et purgatorium eligite,

et post mortem aeternae gaudia vitae gustabitis.

Um., Ig., Mar.:
Beatus ille, qui pro delendis culpis suis
fastidiosa et discordi caproni musica[3]
aures suas fatigabit, castigabit, capronabit;
quoniam post mortem auditui ejus dabitur
gaudium et laetitia in aeternum.
Beatus ille, qui pro delendis culpis suis
asininos capronini[4] tritus patienter audiet,
quia post mortem aeternae gaudia vitae gustabit,
et nectareos angelorum concentus
in fonte voluptatis potabit.

Three angels:
Declaring publicly its unity,
let us venerate the trinity
with equal reverence,
affirming three persons,
differing among themselves
with differences of personality.

The Son is equal to the Father,
nor does the distinct identity
of both deny this;
the Holy Ghost is equal to
Father and Son, and arises
as one with them.

The Father, the Word, the sacred flame,
one God, but all three
having however their own qualities.

One virtue, one power,
one splendor, one light,
one glory in three.

Ig., Mar., Sp.:
O pleasing song, O sweet non-Chaperonian music.

Ig., Mar.:
My life wearies me. Ah, when, my soul,
will you fly to the heavenly homeland
so that you may have your fill of the honeyed nectar of
this song?

Spirit:
O friends, live happily, but not unmindful of death.
For who of you knows whether tomorrow, today,
or in this very hour he may have to die.
Repent and embrace this music of Chaperon;
choose for yourself this music as punishment and
purgatory,
and after death you will taste the joys of eternal life.

Sp., Ig., Mar.:
Blessed is he who, to purge his sins,
will tire, castigate, and chaperonize his ears
with disgusting and discordant, goatish music;
since after death joy and happiness will be given
as an eternal reward for listening to this.

Blessed is he who, to purge his sins, will
patiently listen to this asinine hack-work of Chaperon,
since after death he will taste the joys of eternal life,
and drink the nectar-like harmony of the angels
in the fountain of pleasure.

Notes to the Texts
and Translations

1. *Chara* is used here to facilitate the later pun on Carissimi's name (*chara* or *cara* = "dear, beloved"; *carissimi* = "dearest, most beloved").

2. Similar phonetic playfulness is being applied to Chaperon's name: *capronus* and *chapronus* resemble the Latin *caprinus*, "relating to a goat, goatlike."

3. *Caproni musica* can be interpreted either as "the music of Chaperon" or as "goatish music," which the Spirit implies are one and the same.

4. It is uncertain whether the extra "ni" added to the word *caproni* was intended to imitate the braying of an ass or the bleating of a goat; its effect is disparaging in either case.

Plate I. Marc-Antoine Charpentier, *Orphée descendant aux enfers*,
from autograph manuscript, F-Pn, Rés. Vm^1 259, VI, fol. 11.
(Courtesy Bibliothèque Nationale)

Plate II. *Serenata a tre voci e simphonia,* from autograph manuscript, F-Pn, Rés. Vm¹ 259, VII, fol. 18.
(Courtesy Bibliothèque Nationale)

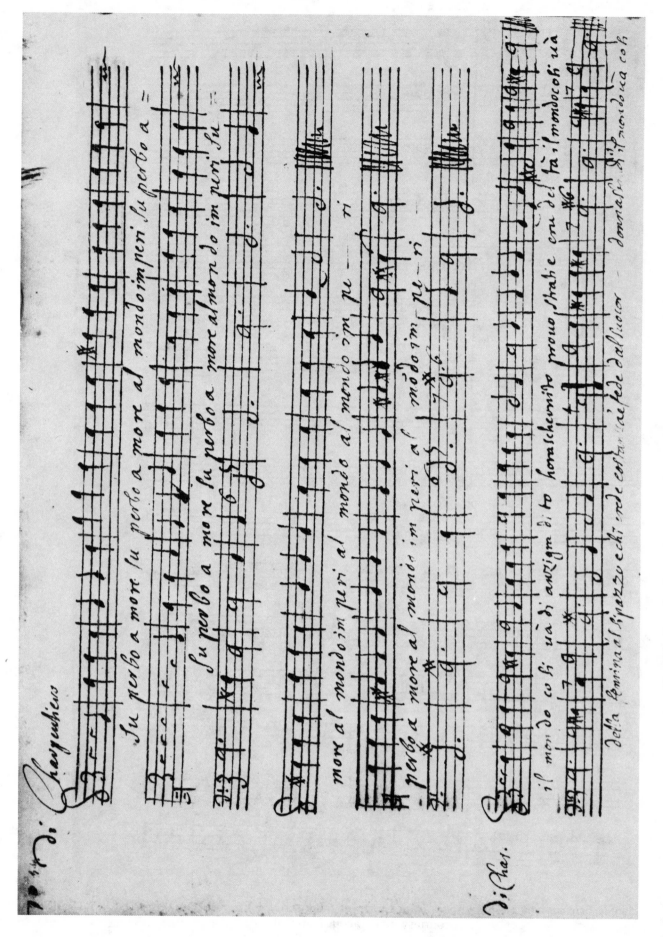

Plate III. *Superbo amore* (top) and *Il mondo così và* (bottom), from F-Pn, Vm⁷ 18, p. 70.
(Courtesy Bibliothèque Nationale)

VOCAL CHAMBER MUSIC

Orphée descendant aux enfers

[I. Prélude]

5

passez sans interruption
au récit d'Orphée sur le viollon

[II.] Récit d'Orphée [sur le viollon]

[III. Air d'Orphée]

9

moy mon ay- ma-ble Eu- ri- di-ce ou_____ lais-sez moy des- cen- dre, ou___ lais- sez

7 6 5   6   7 6   7 6   7 6
#

moy des- cen- dre aux om- bres du___ tré- pas.

7 6   7 6   7 6   6   6   8 9 8 7
                                        6 7 6 5

Hé- las!   Hé- las!   Ou ren- dez moy mon ay- ma- ble Eu-ri-

- di- ce ou_____ lais- sez moy des- cen- dre aux om- - bres du tré-

14

lais- sez moy _ des- cen-dre aux om- bres ____ du tré- pas.

faites icy un petit silence

[IV. Duo]

Ixion

Tantale

Quel-le dou-ce har-mo- ni- e a frap-pé mon or- eil- le et de tous mes tour-

[Basse
continüe]

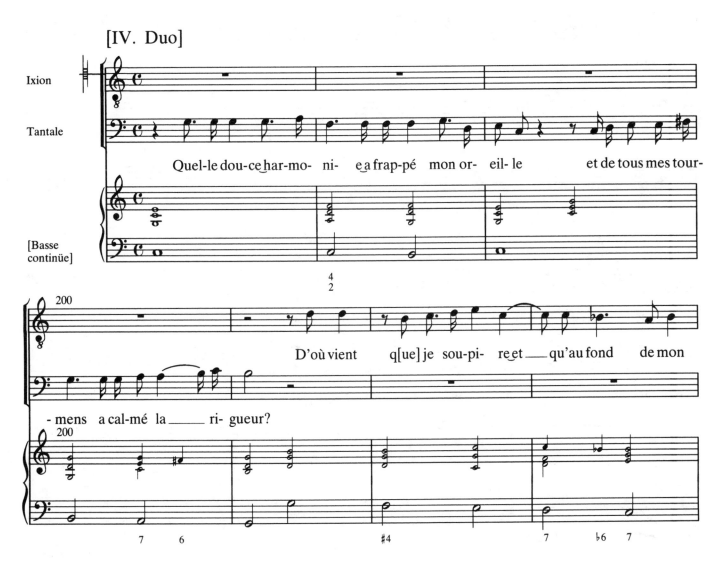

D'où vient q[ue] je sou-pi- re et ___ qu'au fond de mon

- mens a cal-mé la ___ ri- gueur?

16

faites icy une petite pause

[V. Air]

Pr[emier] V[iollon]
[Viollon d']Orph[ée]

S[econ]d V[iollon]

Fl[ûte] à b[ec]

Fl[ûte] alle[mande]

Orph[ée]

[Viole
Basse continuë]

Vos plus grands cri-mi- nels, ron- gés par des vau-tours

sur leurs tris- tes ro- chers, sur leurs tris- tes ro- chers, en- dur-ent moins _ de

peine q'un mal-heu-reux a-mant q[ue]la mort in-hu-mai-ne sé-

-pa-re p[our] ja-mais _____ de ses ten-dres a-mours.

Vos plus grands cri-mi- nels, vos plus grands cri-mi- nels, ron-

-gés par des vau- tours sur leurs tris- tes ro- chers, sur leurs tris- tes ro- chers, en-

-dur- ent moins_ de pei- ne q'un mal- heu-reux a- mant q[ue] la mort in- hu-

22

[VI. Duo et Trio]

[Ixion]

Ne cher-chons plus d'où vient cet-te ten-dres-se qui rem- plit no- tre coeur d'u-ne

[Tantale]

[Basse continüe]

24

- las!   Rien n'est é- gal   au bon-heur des a-   mans,

- las!   Rien n'est é- gal   au bon-heur des a-   mans,

- las!   Rien n'est é- gal   au bon-heur des a-   mans,

27

pour peu q[ue] l'a- mour tou-che u-ne â- me   el- le ne res-sent point tous les   au-tres   tour-

pour peu q[ue] l'a- mour tou-che u-ne â- me   el- le ne res-sent point tous les   au- tres tour-

pour peu q[ue] l'a- mour tou-che u-ne â- me   el- le ne res-sent point tous les   au-tres   tour-

- mens.   Hé- las!   Hé- las!   Rien n'est é- gal   au bon-

- mens.   Hé- las!   Hé- las!   Rien n'est é- gal   au bon-

- mens.   Hé- las!   Hé- las!   Rien n'est é- gal   au bon-

- ne â- me el- le ne res-sent plus tous les au- tres tour- mens.

- ne â- me el- le ne res-sent plus tous les au- tres tour- mens. Rien n'est é-

- ne â- me el- le ne res-sent plus tous les au- tres tour- mens. Hé- las!

Rien n'est é- gal au bon-heur des a- mans, rien n'est é-

- gal au bon-heur des a- mans.

Hé- las! Rien n'est é-

Hé- las!

Rien n'est é-

- gal au bon- heur des a- mans, rien n'est é- gal au bon-heur des a- mans,

- gal au bon- heur des a- mans, rien n'est é- gal au bon-heur des a- mans,

- gal, hé- las! Rien n'est é- gal au bon-heur des a- mans,

pour peu q[ue] l'a- mour tou- che u- ne â- me el- le ne res-sent

pour peu q[ue] l'a- mour tou- che u- ne â- me

pour peu q[ue] l'a- mour tou- che u- ne â- me el- le ne res-sent

plus tous les   au- tres tour- mens,   el- le ne res-sent plus tous les   au- tres   tour-mens.

el- le ne res-sent plus tous les   au-   tres tour- mens.

plus tous les   au-tres   tour- mens,   el- le ne res-sent plus tous les   au-tres   tour-   mens.

fin

Cantate françoise de M. Charpentier

attr. Marc-Antoine Charpentier

cou- léz, _____ cou-léz _____ char-mans ruis-seaux,

cou- léz, cou- léz char-mans ruis-seaux,

por-tés par tout ma tris- te plain- te. Cou-léz, cou-

- léz char-mans ruis-seaux, por-tés par tout ma tris- te plain-

- te,

por- tés par tout, por-tés par tout ma tris- te plain- te.

Pour fuir l'a- mour, le bruit et la con- train- te,

j'es-tois ve- nû dans ce ham- eau; je n'ai-mois rien que mon trou-peau, j'es-tois heu-

-reux, quand la cru-el- le A- min- te m'en-ga- gea dans un li- en nou-

-veau. J'ay dé- cou- vert___ un feu si beau, mais tou- jours dans ses

yeux la froi- deur est dé- pein- te, mais tou- jours dans mon

coeur la froi- deur, la froi- deur est dé- pein- te. Cou-léz, cou- léz___

tout, por-tés par tout ma tris- te plain-te, por-tés par tout,

por-tés par tout ma tris- te plain- te.

Serenata a tre voci e simphonia

Preludio

Choro

Sù sù sù, non dor- mi-te a-man- ti, a- man- ti, sù sù sù, non dor-

Sù sù sù, non dor- mi-te a-man- ti, a- man- ti, sù sù

Sù sù sù, non dor-mi-te a- man- ti, sù sù sù, non dor-

- ge-te, ar de- - te! Ver-go-gno-so, ver- go- [g]no-so è il ri-po-

- ti: ar- de- - te! Ver-go-gno-so, ver- go- gno-so è il ri-po-

- te, pian-ge-te, ar- de- - te! Ver- go-gno-so è il ri-po-

- so: A-mor non vuo-le, A-mor non v[u]o-le, A- mor non

- so: A-mor non vuo-le, A-mor non

- so: A- mor non vuo- le dor- mi-glio- - so cam-

vuo-le dor- mi-glio- so cam- pion ne le sue scho- le.

vuo-le dor- mi-glio- so cam- pion ne le sue scho- le.

- pion dor- mi-glio- so cam- pion ne le sue scho- le.

Sù sù sù, non dor- mi-te a-man- ti, a- man-

Sù sù sù, non dor- mi-te a-man- ti, a- man-

Sù sù sù, non dor-mi- te a-man-

- te, pian- ge- te, so- spi- ra- te, pian- ge- te, ar- de-

- ge- te, so- spi- ra- te, pian- ge- te, ar- de-

- ti: so- - spi- ra- te, pian- ge- te, ar- de-

7   ♮4

- te! Ver- go- gno- so, ver- go- gno- so è il ri- po- so: A- mor non vuo- le,

- te! Ver- go- gno- so, ver- go- gno- so è il ri- po- so: A- mor non

- te! Ver- go- gno- so è il ri- po- so: A- mor non

55

6   5   7 6 5
♭   3 4 4 3

Io non dor-mo, io non ri- po- so,

io non dor-mo, io non ri- po- so, e s'il ciel già s'os- cu- ró cer- can- do _____

vó un più bel so-le en-tro due lu-ci, en-tro due lu-ci as-co- so.

Io non dor-mo, io non ri- po- so, io non dor-mo, io non ri-

- po- so, non ri-po- so, nò, nò, io non dor-mo, io non ri- po- so, e s'il ciel già s'os- cu-

- ró cer- can- do ____ vó, cer- can- do ____ vó un più bel so-le en-tro due

lu-ci, en-tro due lu-ci as-co- so.

[Haute-contre *Alto*]

Io tra pe-ne e tra so- spi- ri,

io tra pe-ne_e tra_so- spi-ri im-mor-tal_____ ser- bo mia fè, e so-no_a me

premio sem- pre_ba- stan-te i miei mar-ti- - ri, i miei mar-ti-

- [ri]. Io tra pe-ne_e tra_so- spi- ri im-mor- tal_____

ser- bo mia   fè, e so-no_a me   pre-mio sem- pre _ ba-   stan-te i miei mar-ti- ri, i

mie- i _ mar- ti-   ri.

[Basse-taille *Bass*]

Il mio cuor, no-bil guer-

- rie- ro, il mio cuor, no- bil guer- rie- ro, nel pe-ri-

- glio, nel pe-ri-glio lie-to stà, _____ nel pe-ri-glio lie-to

[s]tà;   il mio c[u]or, no- bil guer- rie- ro,

il mio c[u]or, no- bil guer- rie- ro,   nel pe-ri-   glio,   nel pe-ri- glio lie- to

stà, _____ nel pe-ri-glio lie-to   stà;

ne bra-mar_____ sà van-to o glo- ria mag-gior del suo pen-sie-

-ro; ne bra-mar_____ sà, ne bra-mar_____ sà van-to o glo- ria mag-

-gior, van-to o glo- ria mag-gior del suo pen-sie- ro, del suo pen-

-sie-   ro.

5 6 5 6 5
3 4 3 4 4 3

[Choro]

Se può dor-mir, se può dor-mir un co- re lie- to e con-

Se può dor- mir un co- re lie- to e con-

Se può dor- mir, se può dor-mir un co- re lie- to e con-

[Superbo amore]

-tà, li- ber- tà, li- ber- tà, li- ber- tà, li- ber- tà!

-tà, li- ber- tà, li- ber- tà, li- ber- tà,_____ li- ber- tà!

[Il mondo così và]

[Dessus
Soprano]

Il mon- do co- sì và: di- an- zi gra- di- to, ho- ra scher-
Del- la fe- mi- na_a'l si, paz-zo_è chi cre- de; co-stan- za_e

[Basse
continüe]

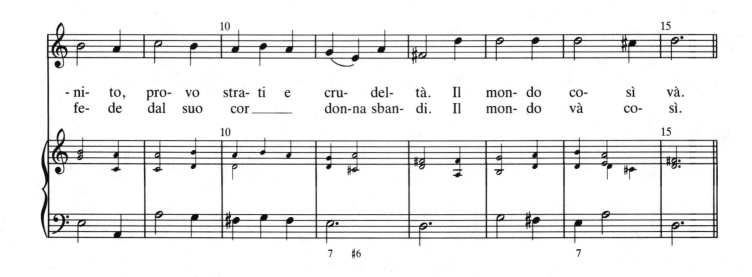

-ni- to, pro- vo stra- ti e cru- del- tà. Il mon- do co- sì và.
fe- de dal suo cor_____ don-na sban- di. Il mon- do và co- sì.

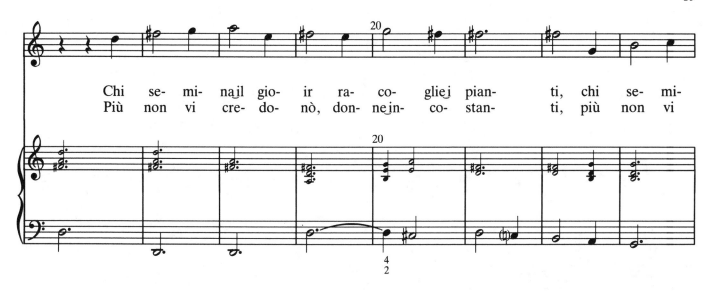

Chi se-mi-na il gio-ir ra-co-glie i pian- ti, chi se-mi-
Più non vi cre-do- nò, don-ne in- co-stan- ti, più non vi

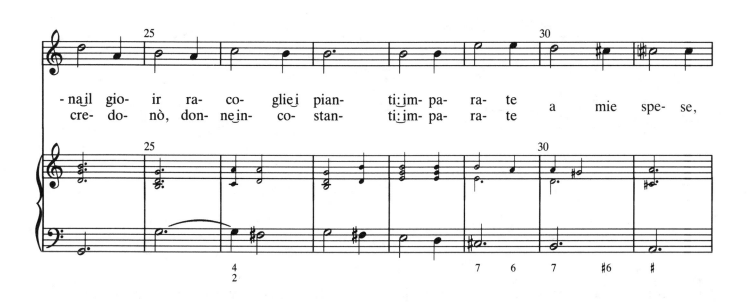

-na il gio-ir ra-co-glie i pian- ti im-pa-ra-te   a mie spe-se,
cre-do- nò, don-ne in- co-stan- ti im-pa-ra- te   a mie spe-se,

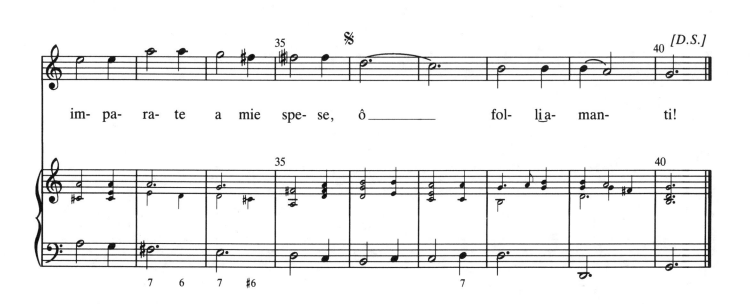

im- pa- ra- te   a mie spe-se, ô_____ fol- lia- man- ti!

Beate mie pene

Duo a doi canti del Sign. Charpentier

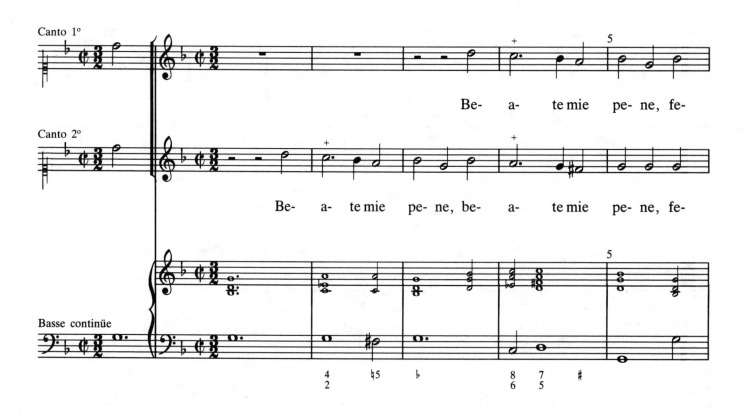

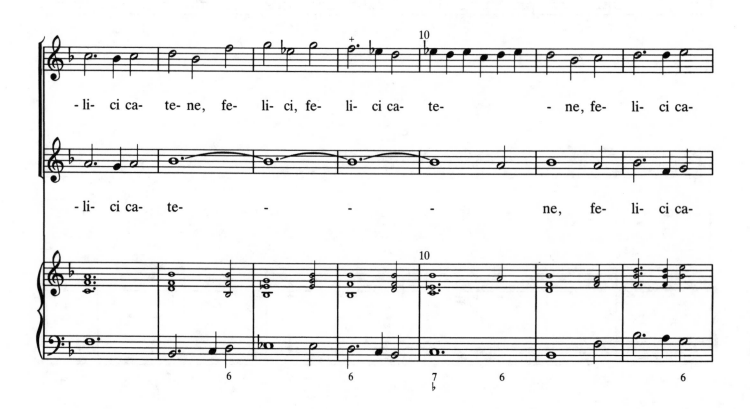

Epitaphium Carpentarij

Interlocutores: Ignatius, Marcellus, Umbra Carpentarij, Tres angeli

Quid au- di-o,

quod mur-mur hor-ri- so-nu[m] si-mul es har-mo-ni-cum au-res me-as pe- pu-lis?

[Marcellus *Bass*]

Quid vi- de-o? Ter-ra tre-mit. Hic la-pis in- hi-at. Hic tu-mu-lus e-vo-mit um-bra[m]. O por-

O por- ten-tum, fu-gi- a- mus, fu-gi- a-mus!

- ten- tum, fu-gi-a- - mus, fu-gi a- - mus!

suivez à l'aise

Umbra [*Alto*]

A- mi- ci, vi-a- to-res, no- li- te ti- me-re, no- li- te ti- me- re. Sis- ti-te

es, o vi-ta, o vi- ta qua[em] bre- vis es.

es, o vi-ta, o vi-ta qua[m]__ bre- vis es.

o vi-ta, o vi- ta qua[em] bre- vis es.

[Umbra]
Mu- si-cus e- ram, in- ter bo- nos a bo-nis, et in-ter ig- na-ros ab ig-nar- is nun-cu-pa-

- tus. Et cum mul-to ma-jor nu-me-rus es-set e- o-rum qui me sper-ne-bant qua[m] qui lau-

- da- bant, mu- si-ca mi-hi par-vus ho-nos sed ma-gnu[m] o- nus __ fu- it; et, si-cut

ter-ris Ca- pro-nus, Cha- pro-nus vo- ca-tur in _ coe- lis.

Do- mi-ne, De-us me-us, quem a-mo, que[m] pos- si- de-o: sa-

-na, pu-ri-fi-ca, san-cti-fi- ca au- res is- to- rum ut pos-sint au- di- re sa- cros an- ge-

- lo- rum con- cen- tus.

Au- di- vit De- us de-pre- ca- ti- o-nem me-am.

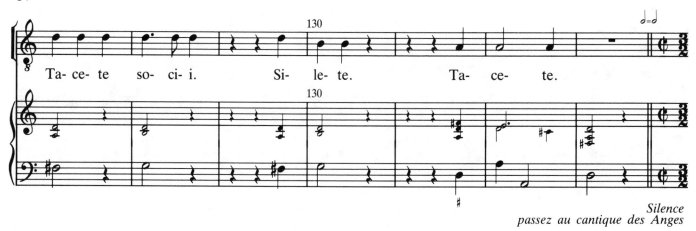

Ta- ce- te so- ci- i. Si- le- te. Ta- ce- te.

Silence
passez au cantique des Anges

Trois Anges qu'on entend et qu'on ne voit point

[Premier Ange]

[Deuxième Ange]

[Troisième Ange]

Pro- fi- ten- tes u- ni- ta- tem, __ ve- ne-

Pro- fi- ten- - tes u- ni- ta- tem, ve- ne-

Pro- fi- ten- - tes u- ni- ta- tem, ve- ne- re- mur

- re- mur tri- ni- ta- tem pa- ri re- ve- ren- ti- a,

- re- mur tri- ni- ta- tem pa- ri re- ve- ren- ti- a,

tri- ni- ta- tem pa- ri re- ve- ren- ti- a,

pro- pri- a. U- na vir- tus, u-num nu- men,

pri- a. U- na vir- tus, u-nu[m] nu- men,

pro- pri- a. U- na vir- tus, u- nu[m] nu- men,

u- nus splen- dor, u-nu[m] lu-men, u-na tri- bus glo- ri- a, _____

u- nus splen- dor, u-nu[m] lu-men, u-na tri- bus glo- ri- a,

u- nus splen- dor, u-nu[m] lu-me[n], u-na tri- bus glo- ri- a,

echo
_____ u-na tri- bus glo- ri- a.

echo
a, _____ u-na tri- bus glo- ri- a.

echo
u- nus splen- dor, u- nu[m] lu-men, u-na tri- bus glo- ri- a.

echo

suivez à l'aise

90

Umbra

O a- mi- ci, vi- vi- te lae- ti, at non im- me- mo- res le- thi.

Quis e- nim ves- trum scit an cras an ho- di- e an hac ip- sa for- si- tan ho- ra sit mo- ri- en-

- dum. Poe- ni- ten- ti- am a- gi- te, ad ca- pro- ni mu- si- cam

cur- ri- te. Hanc in sup- pli- ci- um vo- bis et pur- ga- to- ri- um e- li- gi-

96

-ta- re- os an- ge- lo- rum con- cen- tus in fon- te vo- lup-

-ta- re- os an- ge- lo- rum con- cen- tus in fon- te vo- lup-

fon- te vo- lup- ta- tis po- ta- bit, in fon- te vo- lup-

-ta- tis, in fon- te vo- lup- ta- tis po- ta- bit.

-ta- tis, in fon- te vo- lup- ta- tis po- ta- bit.

-ta- tis, in fon- te vo- lup- ta- tis po- ta- bit.